LOUISVILLE
Then and Now

Louisville Skyline, 1968, by Billy Davis III

LOUISVILLE
Then and Now

Published by

Greater Louisville Inc.
The Metro Chamber of Commerce

in partnership with

Butler Books

and

The University of Louisville
Photographic Archives

Contemporary Photography by
Bill Carner and Christine Leake
with Aron Conaway

Captions and Historical Notes by
James E. Manasco, Delinda S. Buie,
Amy Hanaford Purcell, Thomas L. Owen,
Katherine Burger Johnson and Sharon A. Receveur

Butler Books

© The Courier-Journal, Michael Hayman

Copyright © 2006 by Butler Book Publishing Services, Inc.
Individual photographs held under separate copyright

The historic images contained in this book date from 1889 to 1984 and were taken from the following collections of the University of Louisville Libraries' Photographic Archives:

The Billy Davis, Jr. and Billy Davis III Collections
The Caufield and Shook Collection
The Chamber of Commerce Collection
The Gavin Whitsett Collection
The H.C. Griswold Collection
The L&N Railroad Collection
The Louisville Free Public Library Collection
The Louisville Herald Post Collection
The Martin Schmidt Collection
The Metropolitan Sewer District (MSD) Collection
The R.G. Potter Collection
The Royal Photo Studio Collection
The Terhune Collection

For more information about these and other images in the University of Louisville Photographic Archives, visit the Photo Archives in Ekstrom Library, 2301 South Third Street, Belknap Campus, University of Louisville, Louisville, KY 40292; visit the website: http://library.louisville/ekstrom/special/pa_index.html; or contact the Photo Archives staff by telephone: 502-852-6752, by fax: 502-852-8734, or by email: Special.Collections@louisville.edu.

All Rights Reserved

No part of this book, in whole or in part, may be reproduced by any means without the prior written permission of the copyright holders.

ISBN 1-884532-68-3

Printed in Canada, through Four Colour Imports, Ltd., Louisville, KY

Book design by Scott Stortz

For information, contact the publisher:

Butler Books
P.O.Box 7311, Louisville, KY 40207
502-897-9393/Fax 502-897-9797
billbutler@insightbb.com
www.butlerbooks.com

Courtesy of Bryan Peabody

Greater Louisville Inc.

The Metro Chamber of Commerce

614 West Main Street, Suite 6000
Louisville, KY 40202
502-625-0000

www.greaterlouisville.com

ACKNOWLEDGMENTS

When we first set out to create, for the first time, a book of photographs comparing historic images of the City of Louisville, Kentucky with present-day photographs of the same sites, the project seemed easy enough. On behalf of Greater Louisville Inc. – The Metro Chamber of Commerce – we approached the staff of the University of Louisville Libraries' Photographic Archives to ask them to help us select historic images of Louisville from their renowned collections. Choosing the actual images to feature in this book proved challenging, however, since their combined photographic collections now number over 1.75 million images and thousands begged to be included.

From day one, the devoted, professional staff in UofL's Photographic Archives – James Manasco, Delinda Buie, Bill Carner, Amy Hanaford Purcell, Andy Anderson and Ann Collins; their assistants, Christine Leake and Aron Conaway; and their colleagues in University Archives, Tom Owen and Kathie Johnson – have given generously of their time and talent to support this book project. They join their President, James R. Ramsey, their Provost, Shirley Willihnganz, and their Dean of University Libraries, Hannelore Rader, in supporting UofL's partnership with city leaders and civic organizations like Greater Louisville Inc. on community projects. But they also saw the publication of this book as a unique opportunity to showcase the treasure trove of historic photos in their archive collections.

We are grateful to the team of distinguished historians, archivists and photo archivists at UofL for their months of hard work searching for, scanning and identifying the historic photos featured in this volume. We also want to thank them – and former City of Louisville archivist Sharon Receveur – for writing captions and historical notes for the photographs. Their collective knowledge of Louisville history is impressive, and well-documented in this book. They also consulted previously-published works of colleagues to properly identify some of the images used in this book and, on their behalf, we want to thank those historians – especially George H. Yater, Samuel W. Thomas, John L. Kleber, and Joanne Weeter – for the assistance they and their works provided to our team.

Gathering the historic images was only the first step, however. Bill Carner – a long-time professional photographer and Imaging Manager at UofL's Photographic Archives – offered in the beginning to shoot the "now" photos for this book. Once again, the task was daunting. No one could have imagined how difficult it would be for Bill and his assistants – Christine Leake and Aron Conaway – to find the exact location of each "then" shot, and to capture a photograph that would truly reflect the same content, lighting, angle, etc. as the historic image.

We are grateful to Bill and his staff for their hard work and perseverance getting access to facilities, dodging traffic, waiting for weather to clear, lining up equipment, climbing into place to capture just the right photo. With few exceptions, clearly marked in the book, the "now" photos in this book are Bill's, and we are grateful to him and his staff for sharing their time and talent with us on this project.

We want to thank all the building owners and managers who accommodated Bill's requests for access. We also want to thank all the companies and individuals who helped us locate photos we could not obtain except with their help and who gave us permission to use them: Billy Davis III, Bryan Peabody, Hines, E.ON U.S., Waterfront Development Corporation, Papa John's International, Yum! Brands International, Greater Louisville Inc., Paul Schultz, Bernard Trager at Republic Bank, Jackie Blair at UPS, Megan Robison at GE, Chuck Hoffman at Ford Motor Company, Rande Swann at Louisville International Airport, Cinnamon Jawor at Greater Louisville Convention and Visitors Bureau, Ida Sims at the Public Radio Partnership, Amanda Storment at the Kentucky Exposition Center, Hank Mangeot at BellSouth, Scott Stortz, Mike Maloney, Eric Butler, Sharon Bidwell at the *Courier-Journal* archives, Rick Bell and the Portland Museum. Special thanks as well to our talented graphic designer, Scott Stortz, for once again creating a beautiful book for us.

Most importantly, we want to thank our partners in this publication – President Joe Reagan, Vice Presidents Tracee Troutt and Carmen Hickerson and the team at Greater Louisville Inc.; and President James R. Ramsey, Provost Shirley Willihnganz, University Libraries Dean Hannelore Rader and their staff at the University of Louisville – for their belief in and continuing support of Butler Books and this project.

We hope they are proud of the roles they have played in the publication of this first-time-ever, side-by-side collection of "then and now" photographic images of the City of Louisville, Kentucky.

Familiar images from our past make our present much clearer and help us frame a vision for our future. We hope this book will be enjoyed by people of all ages in 2006 and treasured by generations of Louisvillians to come.

Carol and Bill Butler, Butler Books

"It is very hard to remember that events now long in the past were once in the future."

- Frederic William Maitland

Photo Illustration created by Paul Schultz
Photography by Alliance Photography Group

Caufield and Shook Collection 7048 – circa 1920

The 600 block of West Main Street, then and now.

> *"The farther back you look, the farther forward you are likely to see."*
>
> *- Sir Winston Churchill*

From the President and CEO of Greater Louisville Inc. –

There may be no other city in America that treasures its architectural past more than Louisville, Kentucky. Our city has a long memory and a fondness for not just the buildings that make up its "look," but for the people, traditions and events that lived in or took place inside those buildings. This form of generational continuity is an important facet of Louisville's distinctive character as an immensely livable, friendly and comfortable city.

We fondly remember the bricks and mortar of our landscape, especially as we often still work and play in the same buildings, although perhaps renovated and re-purposed from their original forms. They remain with us, and looking back at them in these pages is akin to looking through a treasured family album.

But "new" happens in Louisville too. As the pictures in this volume attest, new is everywhere you look, from the imaginative renovation of downtown warehouses into living spaces, museums, restaurants and hotels, to new office buildings, hospitals, and residential communities bursting out of the county boundaries. An exciting, progressive vibe rushes through the streets of our river city – attracting new construction and world-class architecture, welcoming new businesses and residents and bringing new opportunities. Things are changing so quickly that it is safe to say that if this book were re-published five years from now, half of it would be entirely new.

So it gives me great pride, on behalf of Greater Louisville Inc. – The Metro Chamber of Commerce – to present simultaneously this side-by-side view of Louisville's venerable past and its dynamic present. We were not able to include photos and stories for all of the historically-significant buildings and businesses we uncovered while researching this book. But the images included, more effectively than words alone, demonstrate how much Louisville has progressed and developed, while retaining its essential charm and beauty. Louisville is an ideal city in that way – big enough to provide a rich, cosmopolitan life in its urban core, yet surrounded by a diverse cluster of neighborhoods and countryside where families can find contentment and put down long roots.

While viewing our past and present, it is just a small leap to imagine our glorious future – a perfect balance, perhaps unique in America, between work and play, old and new, innovation and tradition. It is a future that Greater Louisville Inc. is working hard to achieve.

Joe Reagan
President and CEO
Greater Louisville Inc.

Caufield and Shook Collection 4515 – 1935

The University of Louisville traces its history back to the founding of Jefferson Seminary in 1798. The University's Belknap Campus, named in honor of benefactor William R. Belknap, dates to 1924 when the city bought the campus of the School of Reform on South Third Street. The classically-styled main entrance to Belknap Campus is capped by the University's handsome administration building, Grawemeyer Hall. Originally known as the Administration Building when built in 1926, it was renamed in 1988 for H. Charles Grawemeyer, in honor of his gift establishing five internationally-renowned awards presented annually to scholars in the areas of Education, Improving World Order, Music Composition, Psychology, and Religion. The Grawemeyer Award in Religion is presented jointly with the Louisville Presbyterian Theological Seminary. The University's signature sculpture, "The Thinker" by Auguste Rodin, sits in front of Grawemeyer Hall and has been identified as one of the artist's rare original casts.

"History teaches everything, even the future."

- Alphonse de Lamartine

From the President of the University of Louisville –

The University of Louisville prides itself on being a preeminent metropolitan university and, as such, enjoys partnering with the City of Louisville and civic-minded organizations like Greater Louisville Inc. – The Metro Chamber of Commerce – on important projects like the publication of this exciting new book, *Louisville Then and Now*.

The University of Louisville Libraries are at the heart of our university. Because their primary mission is to support the research and teaching of our students and faculty, our libraries house a wide range of valuable resources, including original source materials – from rare books, manuscripts and archival materials to historic maps and posters. Many of our unique collections document Louisville's business and cultural heritage and provide research opportunities to scholars around the globe, as well as to people of all ages and interests in our community.

The University of Louisville Library's Photographic Archives are one of the great treasures of our university, with holdings now approaching 1.75 million images. They were begun in 1962 as one of the first collections of documentary history photographs in the nation and they now house significant collections of regional and historic photographs, including the R.G. Potter Collection and the rich archives of the Caufield and Shook and Royal Photo Studios Collections. You will enjoy seeing images from those renowned collections and many others from our archives in this beautiful volume of "then and now" photographs – the first of its type to be published in our city.

Popular images from our Photographic Archives have appeared in books, films, documentaries and exhibitions, so readers will recognize in these pages some of their old favorites. Many of our images, however, are being published here for the first time. We hope you enjoy this rare glimpse into some of the treasures awaiting further discovery in the University of Louisville Libraries.

Dr. James R. Ramsey
President
University of Louisville

"Nothing endures but change."

- Heraclitus

The north-facing view from the Iroquois Park Overlook
Caufield and Shook Collection 38242 – 1921

Change is an inevitable fact of urban life. Louisville, like a living organism, has seen landmark buildings come and go. In downtown, for instance, over the past two centuries log structures have given way to modest stone, then to substantial brick buildings, and finally to sleek towers of glass, stone and steel. In an observation that would apply to our modern city, the ancient philosopher Heraclitus observed that, "You cannot step in the same stream twice." Indeed, streetscape change is relentless.

Louisville never wants to be a city with a brand-new look. We take great pride in buildings from the past that have survived to fresh uses, and seldom view the wrecking ball as a friend. Around Louisville, some folks play a parlor game where a building's genealogy is recalled one occupant at a time. Those of us who measure our years by decades persist in telling and re-telling what used to be at a busy intersection or neighborhood's heart, though the buildings themselves may have been torn down years ago.

Louisville Then and Now shows us as we are – a delightful blend of the old and new. These photographs will rekindle regret over landmarks lost, pride in creative re-use, and appreciation for new construction. Beyond that, the volume will whet the appetite for telling what was, and clarifying our taste for what can be.

Thomas L. Owen
Archivist, University of Louisville
Member, Louisville Metro Council

CITY HALL

Northwest Corner of Sixth and Jefferson Streets

Louisville's City Hall, completed in 1873, was originally designed to occupy the entire block of Jefferson between Sixth and Seventh Streets. Only a third of John Andrewartha's elaborate, award-winning building was ever built. The merger of architectural styles reflected the city's merged history as a center for agriculture, commerce and transportation. Stone heads of pigs, cows, donkeys and horses peer from above the second story windows of City Hall, and a train over the building's main entrance signals Louisville's post-Civil War aspirations as the gateway to the south. The clock tower on City Hall originally served as a fire watchtower. Shortly after the building opened, however, the watchtower itself caught fire and was replaced by the current clocktower.

Caufield and Shook Collection 7002 – circa 1915

Since the 2003 merger of the City of Louisville and Jefferson County into the new city of Louisville Metro, City Hall houses metro government offices, including the legislative chambers and offices of the 26 members of the Louisville Metro Council.

THE JEFFERSON COUNTY COURTHOUSE / LOUISVILLE METRO HALL

Jefferson Street between Fifth and Sixth Streets

Construction of the Jefferson County Courthouse was begun in 1835. It is Louisville Metro's oldest public building. Engineer Albert Fink completed his adaptation of Gideon Shryock's original design in 1860, among other things adding cast iron elements to the building's walkways, stairs and rotunda. Once the Courthouse was complete, some city boosters believed Louisville could become Kentucky's state capital. Although critics referred to the building in 1860 as "an elephantine monstrosity," and in 1926 as "that antiquated pile," citizens defeated an attempt in the 1940s to demolish the building.

Caufield and Shook Collection 127111 – 1933

Today the building is recognized as one of the most important Greek Revival structures in the United States. Since city/county merger in 2003, the Jefferson County Courthouse has been called Louisville Metro Hall. It now houses the offices of Louisville Metro's Mayor and the Jefferson County Clerk. A huge statue of Thomas Jefferson stands at the base of the front steps of Louisville Metro Hall.

On the two southern corners of the building's lot stand a statue of Louisville's namesake—King Louis XVI of France—and a memorial to Louisville's fallen soldiers of World War II. In the photograph above, dozens of colorful automobiles in town for the National Street Rod Convention gather in front of Louisville Metro Hall for an official welcome to Louisville.

LOUISVILLE METRO HALL / STATUE OF THOMAS JEFFERSON

500 Block of West Jefferson Street

Thomas Jefferson was the governor of Virginia when the town of Louisville was chartered in 1780. Kentucky was a part of the Commonwealth of Virginia until 1789. In 1899, philanthropist Isaac Bernheim gave the city a Moses Ezekiel statue of Thomas Jefferson. It stands in front of Louisville Metro Hall, formerly the Jefferson County Courthouse, facing south. One of the "civic angels" surrounding the Liberty Bell on which Jefferson is standing is symbolically tearing up old governance documents that became obsolete after the American Revolution. In this 1921 photo, the statue is overlooking the former extension of Center Street (Armory Place) to Jefferson Street, now closed by the construction of Jefferson Square Park. Across the park stands the Jefferson County jail, designed by D. X. Murphy, that opened in 1905, receiving praise for its sanitary and mechanical innovations.

Caufield and Shook Collection 38356 – 1921

Today the former jail has been renovated to serve as government offices and the Jefferson County law library. Jefferson Square Park provides a green space used for alfresco lunches and strolls by downtown workers. It often serves as the venue for city-wide celebrations such as Light Up Louisville and memorial observances. Park features include a fleur-de-lis fountain and memorials to fallen police and firefighter heroes. During the holidays, the city's traditional holiday tree is temporarily erected over the site of the fountain. To the park's right stands the Louis D. Brandeis Hall of Justice at Sixth and Jefferson Streets.

FIRE STATION NUMBER 2 / SINKING FUND BUILDING

600 block of West Jefferson Street

Fire Station Number 2, once Louisville's chief fire station, opened at 619 West Jefferson Street in 1891. In this 1920 photograph, the west tower still features an impressive dome, protecting the bell that rang alarms for the city. The demands of modern firefighting led to the construction of a new Louisville Fire Department headquarters building in 1938, and the bell and the dome disappeared as the building was adapted for use by Louisville city government.

Caufield and Shook Collection 33181 – 1920

Now housing Louisville Metro government offices, the building nonetheless still recalls its original purpose. The wide-arched entries, built as doors for fire engines, are below *bas relief* representations of 19th-century Fire Chief Ed Hughes and Assistant Chief Benjamin Bache. The façade is decorated with ornaments depicting objects that even today constitute firefighting apparatus—helmets, axes, and hoses.

LOUISVILLE METRO POLICE DEPARTMENT

Louisville trustees appointed five police officers, then known as town watchmen, in 1806. While the ranks of those first officers grew with the city, the police reported first to the trustees, then to the mayor, before the position of Chief of Police was established in 1856. The 1889 image above shows a professional, disciplined force standing in front of Louisville's City Hall.

R.G. Potter Collection - 709.1 - 1889

R.G. Potter Collection 705 – circa 1928

The class of 2006 stands with Chief Robert C. White and Mayor Jerry Abramson in front of Memorial Auditorium, Fourth and Kentucky Streets, following their graduation ceremony. These new officers joined the Louisville Metro Police Department, formed by the merger of the Louisville and Jefferson County police departments in 2003. Over 1,200 officers and 300 civilians now work for the LMPD.

(Opposite page, and right) Although Louisville Metro Police Officers now employ state-of-the-art technology and vehicles in their work, they also still use both bicycles and horses, when appropriate, to help keep peace and order in the city.

Photos courtesy of Louisville Metro Police Department

CITIZENS FIDELITY BANK / PNC BANK

500 Block of West Jefferson Street

In 1858, the Commonwealth of Kentucky extended a charter to a new Merchants Deposit Bank that changed its name to Citizens Bank five years later. Known after 1944 as Citizens Fidelity Bank & Trust Company, the institution played a pivotal role in the development of Louisville. In 1971, the bank contributed Citizens Plaza, still one of the city's tallest buildings, to the Louisville skyline. The Jefferson Club occupies the 29th floor of the tower, providing diners with a spectacular view of the city.

Chamber of Commerce Collection 82.15.109 – 1972

In 1987, Citizens Fidelity Bank & Trust Company was absorbed by nationally-prominent PNC Financial Corporation and today operates as PNC. Across Liberty Street from PNC tower is the former U.S. Federal Reserve building, which was purchased by the City and now serves as the headquarters of MetroSafe – Louisville Metro's emergency communications system.

LIBERTY NATIONAL BANK / BANK ONE / JPMORGAN CHASE BANK

400 Block of West Jefferson Street

Liberty National Bank, later Bank One, now JPMorgan Chase, is distinguished as the oldest bank still operating in Kentucky. Chartered in 1854 as the German Insurance Company, the banking functions separated in 1872 and became known as the German Insurance Bank. In 1918, during World War I, the bank joined other regional institutions to express patriotism through a name change.

Royal Photo Studio Collection 17256.01 – 1960

First Louisville National Bank, then the Louisville Trust Company, later United Kentucky Bank, now JPMorgan Chase—a bank has stood on this corner of Baxter at Highland Avenue since 1922.

R.G. Potter Collection 3978 – circa 1930

LOUISVILLE THEN AND NOW

Liberty Insurance Bank became Liberty National Bank in 1935 and remained a financial force in Louisville until it was purchased by Bank One Corporation in 1994. In 2004, Bank One Corporation was acquired by New York City-based JPMorgan Chase & Co. Since 2005, Louisville's oldest financial institution bears the name Chase.

Today, the banking corner at Baxter and Highland Avenues is a Chase Bank, serving the residents of this lively Highlands neighborhood of restaurants, pubs and nightspots.

JEFFERSON HOTEL / MARRIOTT HOTEL / KENTUCKY INTERNATIONAL CONVENTION CENTER

200 Block of West Jefferson Street

Hotels have played a prominent role in the history of this site at Second and Jefferson Streets. Pictured here in a 1934 photograph, the Jefferson Hotel contributed to what the Louisville Convention and Publicity League estimated, in 1923, as accommodations for 7,000 persons available in the city. In 2005, a Marriott Hotel opened on the site previously occupied by the Jefferson.

Caufield and Shook Collection 135882 – 1934

The new Louisville Marriott Downtown Hotel, with its 450 guest rooms and 50,000 square feet of meeting space, contributes to the current 17,000 rooms available for tourists and conventioneers in downtown Louisville. Visitors spend $1.2 billon annually in Louisville Metro. Just north of the new hotel is the Kentucky International Convention Center, a 300,000-square-foot facility constructed by the state to host conventions and events. The popular venue, which contains 52 meeting rooms under one roof, is connected to more than 3700 hotel rooms via pedways throughout downtown. The building also houses the Kentucky World Trade Center and the offices of Sister Cities of Louisville, Inc.

THE LEVY BROTHERS BUILDING

Northeast Corner of Third and Market Streets

Henry and Moses Levy opened Levy Brothers on the corner of Third and Market Streets in 1893, and outfitted Louisville men and boys from that location until 1979. The building was one of the first in Louisville with electric lights. The Louisville colloquialism "Lit up like Levy's" referenced the Levy Brothers' exuberant use of lights on the façade and window displays.

Royal Photo Studio Collection 50876 – circa 1939

In 1984, investors took advantage of a Federal Investment Tax Credit program for updating core inner city buildings. The success of Levy's renovation set a precedent for the adaptive reuse of many of Louisville's 19th-century buildings. Now an Old Spaghetti Factory restaurant franchise occupies the lower floors, with offices and condominiums above.

GREATER LOUISVILLE SAVINGS & BUILDING ASSN / U.S. BANK

400 Block of West Market Street

Greater Louisville Savings & Building Association, located at 419 West Market, was one of a number of Louisville-based savings and loan banks supporting growth in personal savings and home construction in the decades after World War I and World War II. Changes in Kentucky's banking laws beginning in the 1970s led to most of these savings and loans being absorbed by larger banks.

Caufield and Shook Collection 31243 – 1920

Today, this block of Market Street at Fourth Street, now known as One Financial Square, is still a banking center—the local headquarters for U.S. Bank. Currently, a banner depicting the running of the Kentucky Derby hangs from the building, one of the enormous vinyl banners being produced by USA Image Technologies, Inc. and placed on buildings around town by the Greater Louisville Pride Foundation.

GOLDBERG'S / HERMAN STRAUS & SONS / AEGON TOWER

Southwest Corner of Fourth and Market Streets

In 1927, Morris Goldberg and his sons Louis and Max worked as merchant tailors at Fourth and Market Streets. The building's open windows provided climate control in the days before air-conditioning. West on Market, Herman Straus & Sons operated a department store, boasting, "Where a dollar does its duty."

Caufield and Shook Collection 83853 – 1927

Today, the Aegon Tower (formerly known as Providian Center) stands as the tallest building in Louisville and in Kentucky. The tower, built under the leadership of the insurance and finance giant's CEO, Irving Bailey, was completed in 1993.

Photo courtesy of Hines

GERMAN BANK BUILDING / VINCENZO'S

Northwest Corner of Fifth and Market Streets

The German Bank Building was designed by Louisville architect D.X. Murphy to reflect the seriousness of its purpose. While other Louisville banks with German roots responded to the conflict of World War I by changing their names, the German Bank instead joined the National Bank of Kentucky and, in 1919, moved offices to Fifth and Main Streets. The impressive edifice became the home of the Federal Reserve Bank through World War II, when the dramatic increase in war bonds business and a resulting doubling of staff led to a move into a new building at Fifth and Liberty Streets in 1958.

Royal Photo Studio Collection 5021 – circa 1939

Humana, Inc. purchased the Federal Reserve Building in 1983 and converted a portion of the building into a conference center and fitness facility. The majority of the building, however, provides elegant space for one of Louisville's most celebrated restaurants, Vincenzo's.

The colorful horse standing outside the entrance to Vincenzo's is one of 223 artfully decorated life-size horses that were produced by local artists for Louisville's Gallopalooza public art project. The horses were auctioned off to raise money for Brightside, Louisville Metro's beautification program, and now appear throughout the city—most often outside the entrances of their sponsors' homes or businesses.

LOUISVILLE TRUST COMPANY / FIRST TRUST CENTRE

Southwest Corner of Fifth and Market Streets

In 1891, Louisville Trust Company opened a handsome seven-story structure on the southwest corner of Fifth and Market Streets. Louisville architects Maury and Dodd employed a popular architectural style known as Richardsonian Romanesque, after Boston architect Henry Hobson Richardson. In 1931, the Great Depression forced Louisville Trust Bank, which by then had absorbed the business of Louisville National Bank, to close. Backed by support of Louisville business leaders, the bank was able to reopen after only one year.

Caufield and Shook Collection 51726 – 1923

In 1972, Louisville Trust Bank moved to West Main Street, and the historic building was adapted for use as public offices, including a driver's license bureau. In 1985, a group of investors known as First Trust Restoration Partnership purchased the building and surrounding structures and renovated them into professional office space. Stock Yards Trust Company now occupies the first floor of First Trust Centre.

THE SNEAD BUILDING / GLASSWORKS

800 Block of West Market Street

The buildings housing the Market Street Architectural Iron Foundry, then the Snead and Company Iron Works, provided cast iron building fronts and manhole covers for Louisville and other cities across the nation. After a fire in 1898, the Snead Company commissioned a new "first-class fireproof building," which opened in 1909.

R.G. Potter Collection 4271.02 – 1935

This construction befits the building's current use, following its renovation in 2000, for the high-heat applications of the Glassworks art glass studio. The multi-use facility also houses galleries, offices, loft apartments and condominiums, and the Jazz Factory, a favorite night spot. The banner of Louisville sculptor Ed Hamilton is one of a number of large format images of famous Louisvillians produced by USA Image Technologies, Inc. and The Greater Louisville Pride Foundation, now hanging on buildings throughout the community.

BOURBON STOCK YARDS / STOCK YARDS BANK

1000 Block of East Main Street

A large tract of land along the Ohio River east and south of Louisville was first annexed by the city in 1827 and began to be populated by German immigrants shortly thereafter. Butchering became a primary occupation in this neighborhood, since it had been banned from the central area of Louisville. The locale provided easy transportation for cattle via what is now Frankfort Avenue and Story Avenue—once called "Cattle Baron Road." This area, which became known as Butchertown, was also ideal for the establishment of meatpacking operations because the proximity of Beargrass Creek provided for the convenient elimination of processing waste. After Louisville's devastating 1937 flood, businesses began to relocate to higher ground. That, coupled with the isolation of the eastern part of the area by the construction of Interstate 64 in the 1960s, caused the gradual decline of Butchertown's commercial prominence.

Caufield and Shook Collection 50443 – 1923

Always a lively residential area, the Butchertown neighborhood has recently enjoyed a renaissance. A new wave of young artists and professionals who are moving into the neighborhood appreciate the area's history and its closeness to downtown. The Home of the Innocents, established in 1880 as an emergency shelter and home for abused, neglected, and medically fragile children, has built a new campus on the site of the old Bourbon Stock Yards while leaving the old entrance intact. Stock Yards Bank and Trust Company, which opened in 1904 across the street from the Bourbon Stock Yards, is one of Louisville's few remaining locally-owned financial institutions. Stock Yards Bank has grown to include offices and branches across the region and has expanded into the renovated offices of The Bourbon Stock Yards.

BRINLY-HARDY / LOUISVILLE SLUGGER FIELD

400 Block of East Main Street

This brick and limestone structure was built in 1902. Shared by the Big Four (Cleveland, Cincinnati, Chicago and St. Louis) and Chesapeake & Ohio railroads, this was one of many depots supporting Louisville's position as a prominent north-south railroad traffic link. The large arches allowed freight cars to enter for unloading inside the depot. Beginning in the 1950s, the depot served as a shipping warehouse for Brinly-Hardy, one of the South's premier manufacturers of plows and farming equipment. In 1998 significant portions of the building underwent renovation and modification to create a new home for the Louisville Bats, the Triple-A affiliate of the Cincinnati Reds.

Top photo, Caufield and Shook Collection 59301 – 1924

Financed through a unique partnership among the Louisville Bats, the City and a number of civic and private supporters, the $27.8 million Louisville Slugger Field opened in 2000. Its retro-classic design and prized position on Louisville's transformed waterfront have earned it praise as one of the most exciting and attractive minor league baseball parks in the country. Fans can enjoy watching Bats baseball games from any of the stadium's 13,000 seats or 32 luxury suites, or from a family picnic area in the rear of the stadium. A statue of Louisville native Pee Wee Reese greets visitors as they enter the ballpark from East Main Street.

Billy Davis III photo 240568 – R1 – 5

East Main Street, Looking West

400 Block of East Main Street

In addition to Louisville Slugger Field, the former Brinly-Hardy building now houses Park Place Restaurant and Browning's Restaurant and Brewery and serves as a site for a variety of civic events and exhibitions. The view looking west from Brinly-Hardy in the 1930s shows a Main Street devoted to the kind of factories and industrial businesses that were a traditional part of the landscape east of Preston Street.

R.G. Potter Collection 1825 – circa 1930

Today's west-facing view shows an entirely different picture: new, architecturally-interesting buildings like Preston Pointe, imaginative renovations of classic structures, and a reinvigorated skyline along the Main Street corridor.

LOUISVILLE PUBLIC WAREHOUSE COMPANY / E-MAIN

100 Block of East Main Street

Built in 1889 for Louisville Public Warehouse Company, the building at the northwest corner of Main at Brook Street stored a variety of manufactured goods produced in or shipped through Louisville. Louisville Public Warehouse Company, now a national company with corporate offices on Progress Boulevard in Louisville, even offered a "special warehouse for household effects," and a bonded facility for whiskey. Belknap Hardware operated one of its own many warehouses just west, toward First Street. Humana purchased Belknap Hardware and the buildings, and in 2000 announced plans, with city and state funding, to renovate the Clock Tower building. Now offering 154,000 square feet of office space, the Clock Tower is at the heart of the district now know as eMain.

Martin Schmidt Collection 98.09.112 – circa 1956

Begun in 1999 as a collaboration between the City of Louisville and private property owners, eMain, as it came to be known, was committed to transforming the area bordered by the Ohio River, East Market Street, the Clark Memorial Bridge and Interstate 65—the eMain district—into a bustling, mixed-use, vibrant community within a community. In 2000, Louisville Mayor David Armstrong convened a meeting of property owners, electronic business leaders, venture capitalists, educators, technology professionals and others to produce a report detailing a vision for the area and laying out a plan to create this "urban village" within downtown. Renovation of the Clock Tower building by Humana became the catalyst for the future transformation of eMain into a thriving commercial and residential neighborhood. The Enterprise Center, located on the first floor, houses the Enterprise Corporation and the Greater Louisville Small Business Development Center, which offer assistance to entrepreneurs and small business owners.

George Rogers Clark Memorial Bridge

Second and Main Streets

After nearly a decade of debate, construction of the Louisville Municipal Bridge began in the middle of the Ohio River in 1928 and proceeded with cantilevered derricks moving toward the south and north shores. On October 29, 1929, the same week as the Stock Market crash, President Herbert Hoover dedicated the bridge as the Ohio River's first span designed exclusively for automobiles. During World War II, Louisville residents traveled the bridge each day to work at several Clark County, Indiana war production factories. The accumulation of tolls allowed the bridge to retire its debt early. The structure, renamed the George Rogers Clark Memorial Bridge after Louisville's legendary founder, is often referred to as the Second Street Bridge.

Caufield and Shook Collection 252863 – 1950

Today the George Rogers Clark Memorial Bridge still serves its original purpose as a bridge across the Ohio River to Jeffersonville, Indiana. It is also a popular destination for lunch-time runners and a dramatic staging site for the annual launch of the Kentucky Derby Festival's "Thunder Over Louisville" fireworks display. Future plans for the northwest corner of Second and Main Streets call for a $450 million multi-purpose arena, hotel and retail complex to be constructed on the riverfront, just west of the Clark Memorial Bridge.

BANK OF LOUISVILLE / ACTORS THEATRE OF LOUISVILLE

300 Block of West Main Street

Built in Greek Revival style, this landmark building between Third and Fourth Streets on the south side of West Main Street was constructed around 1837 and was known as the Bank of Louisville Building. The massive Ionic columns spoke volumes about sturdy classicism and financial integrity. Its graceful exterior framed a domed banking room with a coffered ceiling.

Chamber of Commerce Collection 1982.15.69 – circa 1969

Since its restoration in 1972, led by current Brown-Forman Chairman Owsley Brown II and his wife Christina Lee Brown, the building has been the home of Actors Theatre of Louisville. ATL has remained one of America's most respected and imaginative theater companies for nearly 35 years. It has hosted the Humana Festival of New American Plays—an annual event drawing theater lovers, producers, agents and critics from all over the world to Louisville—for 30 years. ATL has expanded to neighboring buildings, creating spaces to its east and south for offices, parking and the 627-seat Pamela Brown Auditorium. The former bank building has become the theater's lobby entrance.

PRESTON HOTEL / E.ON U.S.

Third and Main Streets

In this circa 1912 photograph, the Preston Hotel, along with its café and saloon, occupied the southeast corner of Third and Main Streets. By 1920, Louisville's business district had moved toward Broadway and the hotel closed. Vacant for decades, the site provided an ideal footprint for the 1989 construction of the new headquarters of the Louisville Gas and Electric (LG&E) Company. LG&E can trace its origins back to 1838 when a group of investors formed Louisville Gas and Water and provided gas-fired street lights to the city. In 1913, Louisville Gas, Louisville Lighting and Kentucky Heating merged to create Louisville Gas and Electric.

Caufield and Shook Collection 7047 – circa 1912

Now owned by E.ON U.S., LG&E serves more than 394,000 electric customers and 321,000 natural gas customers over a service area of 700 square miles. The building is one of the proud icons of Louisville's skyline. At night, the rooftop's signature blue-green lights are reminiscent of the color of a gas flame.

Photo courtesy of E.ON U.S.

LOUISVILLE TRUST BANK / BB&T / ONE RIVERFRONT PLAZA

Northwest Corner of Fourth and Main Streets

The building known as One Riverfront Plaza opened at 401 West Main Street in 1972, the same year as the Galt House just to its north. It originally provided a new headquarters for Louisville Trust Bank, which relocated from its historic location at Fifth and Market. It later housed a branch of Bank One, but now bears the logo of BB&T, which acquired the Bank of Louisville in 2002.

Chamber of Commerce Collection 82.15.137 – 1974

One Riverfront Plaza is now home to Louisville's main branch of BB&T and a variety of businesses and law firms. The top floors of the building are occupied by the Greater Louisville Convention and Visitors Bureau and the Greater Louisville Sports Commission.

AMERICAN LIFE BUILDING

Northeast Corner of Fifth and Main, at the Belvedere

For centuries, the buildings on Main Street stood shoulder-to-shoulder on the flat, high ground above the Louisville waterfront behind them. Bullitt Street ran north to Louisville's historic wharf between Fourth and Fifth Streets. This view of the northeast corner of Fifth and Main Streets shows a slope down to River Road. Today the site is completely transformed, with broad steps rising up to Louisville's Belvedere and a corner dominated by important 20th-century architecture.

Caufield and Shook Collection 146383 – 1936

The year 2006 marks the 100th anniversary of Dinwiddie Lampton, Sr.'s founding the company that ultimately became the American Life and Accident Insurance Company of Kentucky. His son, Dinwiddie Lampton, Jr., acquired several properties along the 400 block of West Main Street in the late 1960s (including the first lot ever surveyed in Louisville) and, with his daughter Nana, hired the firm of architect Mies Van Der Rohe to design a new headquarters for their firm. The building is positioned on its lot to link Louisville's Belvedere with Main Street and to provide ample pedestrian access to both.

BELVEDERE

Main Street, Between Fourth and Sixth Streets

The Bartholomew Plan, a 1932 civic development project, envisioned creation of a public open space for civic events and recreation. Construction was delayed first by the Great Depression, then again by World War II. Reynolds Metals Company took up the cause in the 1960s but found their plans challenged by the construction of Interstate 64 along the Ohio River. Finally, championed by Louisville architects Lawrence Melillo and Jasper Ward, the plan came to fruition in 1973. Louisville's Belvedere—with its fountains, sculptural details and at one time even an outdoor ice skating rink—offered an architecturally interesting venue for Louisville celebrations. The new public space, located between Fourth and Sixth Streets north of Main Street, was named the "Belvedere" because of its "beautiful view" overlooking the Ohio River.

Chamber of Commerce Collection 1982.15.94 – 1975

Renovated in 1998, Louisville's Belvedere now boasts new fountains, waterfalls and water features surrounding an open plaza that provides public space for concerts, international festivals and other events. In addition to a statue of the city's founder, George Rogers Clark, designed by Felix de Weldon, the site now also incorporates an Ed Hamilton sculpture of York, the African-American slave who participated in the Lewis and Clark Expedition.

THE KENTUCKY CENTER

500 Block of West Main Street

Caufield and Shook Collection 186777 – 1942

Running parallel to the waterfront, Main Street was one of Louisville's first streets, with hotels for river travelers and warehouses for goods arriving by boat. Cast iron building fronts, many manufactured in Louisville, allowed maximum natural light. Main Street's array of cast iron buildings, dating back to the 1850s, is one of the world's largest groups of these historic structures.

Though their preservation is a priority, there have been architectural additions to the street that have replaced existing structures. One of them is the magnificent Kentucky Center (formerly Kentucky Center for the Arts), which was built on Main between Fifth and Sixth Streets in 1983.

While the Louisville Ballet, the Louisville Orchestra and the Kentucky Opera Association call the Kentucky Center home, the Whitney and Bomhard theatres and other spaces in the Center offer venues for an even broader range of local and touring companies. In addition to housing performing arts and Jarfi's, a popular restaurant, the Center displays permanent installations of works by extraordinary artists such as Louise Nevelson, Alexander Calder, Joan Miro, and Jean Dubuffet.

Today, the glass facade of the Kentucky Center on the northeast corner of Sixth and Main Streets reflects the 19th-century buildings opposite, a reminder of warehouses that once occupied the site where the Center now stands. Warehouses and retail buildings also flourished on the north side of Main. The Otis Hidden Company, pictured here in 1951, provided wholesale rugs, linoleum, kitchen appliances and window shades. Three decades later, in 1983, the Kentucky Center opened on this site and instantly became the literal and figurative center for performing arts in Kentucky.

Caufield and Shook Collection 261121–1951

FIRST NATIONAL BANK / NATIONAL CITY BANK

Southeast corner of Fifth and Main Streets

National City Bank, Kentucky traces its roots back to 1863 and The First National Bank of Louisville, chartered as the first national bank in the south. In 1910, the bank was absorbed by the Kentucky Title Savings Bank and Trust, but retained its historic name. During the Great Depression, First National Bank of Louisville, acting for the public good, took over the assets and liabilities of the failed First National Bank of Kentucky, then the Commonwealth's largest bank. Known simply as First National, the bank continued growth with the affiliated First Kentucky National Corp.

Billy Davis, Jr. photo 82.15.105 – 1972

First National Bank constructed a new 39-story headquarters at Fifth and Main in 1972. Known as National City Tower since National City Corp. acquired First National in 1988, the structure still holds a prominent place in Louisville's ever-changing skyline.

© *The Courier-Journal, Michael Hayman*

UNITED STATES TRUST COMPANY / HUMANA BUILDING

Southwest Corner of Fifth and Main Streets

In 1955, the United States Trust Company advertised "Complete Banking Services" at 500 West Main Street. Commonwealth Life Insurance Company occupied the top floor with a West Office Annex but positioned its headquarters on Broadway, Louisville's center of commerce during the 1950s.

Caufield and Shook Collection 289529 – 1956

The southwest corner of Fifth and Main Streets is now the home of Humana Inc. Founded as Extendicare in the 1960s, Louisville-based Humana has provided a range of health care services and has supported charitable causes across the country and internationally since 1961. To promote Louisville and to help revitalize Main Street, Humana held a high-profile design competition when planning its new corporate headquarters in 1982. Winning architect Michael Graves incorporated the site's history, the neighboring cast iron buildings, the bridges, boats and the flow of the Ohio River into his design. Upon its completion in 1985, the Humana headquarters brought a fresh look to Louisville's skyline. Since then, the building has been credited with inspiring post-modern architecture across the globe.

Photos courtesy of Humana, Inc.

CARTER DRY GOODS / LOUISVILLE SCIENCE CENTER

700 Block of West Main Street

Except for a brief period during the Civil War, Carter Dry Goods served as Louisville's premier purveyor of wholesale dry goods from 1854 to 1954. The company moved into this spacious four-story building in the 700 block of West Main Street in 1878. Carter Dry Goods continued to be locally-owned until 1954, when it was sold to an out-of-town firm and moved from downtown.

Caufield and Shook Collection 43348 – 1922

In 1977, the City of Louisville purchased the Carter Dry Goods building and renovated it to become the Museum of Natural History and Science, and also to provide space for some city government offices. Several of the museum's core exhibits, including a pair of stuffed polar bears, were formerly housed in the Louisville Free Public Library's Museum. A few of the artifacts and natural history specimens date even further back to the 19th-century collections of the Louisville Polytechnic Society. Renamed and now organized as its own non-profit institution, the Louisville Science Center occupies the entire building and includes Louisville's first IMAX movie theater.

WHAYNE SUPPLY COMPANY /
THE LOUISVILLE SLUGGER MUSEUM AND FACTORY

800 Block of West Main Street

Established in 1913, Whayne Supply sold construction supplies and equipment from this old tobacco warehouse at the corner of Eighth and Main Streets from 1928 forward. This view is from 1956. The neighboring Kentucky Tent & Awning Company supplied tents, tarpaulins and flags. As its business grew, Whayne Supply moved to much larger quarters at 1400 Cecil Avenue in West Louisville.

Caufield and Shook Collection 295453 – 1953

In 1996, the former Whayne Supply building was transformed into a new home for Hillerich and Bradsby's Louisville Slugger Museum and Factory. Construction of the new facility brought Hillerich and Bradsby back home to Louisville after over 20 years of manufacturing Louisville Slugger bats across the river in Jeffersonville, Indiana. John A. "Bud" Hillerich turned his first bat—for Louisville Eclipse player Pete Browning—at the Hillerich family business in 1884. Within a decade the Louisville Slugger had become a registered trademark. In 1905, the Louisville Slugger made history as the first endorsed sports product when Honus Wagner had his autograph burned onto his bats. Baseball greats Ty Cobb, Babe Ruth and Ted Williams carried on the tradition of autographed Louisville Sluggers, an honor now bestowed also on baseball-loving dignitaries. In 1916, Hillerich and Bradsby launched a line of PowerBilt golf clubs. Over the next 80 years, the Hillerich & Bradsby Company manufactured a range of sports equipment, as well as armaments during World War II. The world's largest baseball bat (120 feet tall, 68,000 pounds) rests imposingly in front of the building where the Louisville Slugger Museum and Factory welcomes visitors to watch actual production in the adjacent factory.

LOUISVILLE SEED COMPANY / FRAZIER INTERNATIONAL HISTORY MUSEUM

Northeast Corner of Ninth and Main Streets

This handsome building at the corner of Ninth and Main Streets housed seed wholesalers for much of its early history. Louisville Seed, shown in this 1936 photograph, replaced Hardin, Hamilton, & Lewman Wholesale Seeds and was among the few businesses on Main Street able to survive the 1937 flood. A maker of blue jeans, at one time one of Louisville's important exports, also once occupied the building. In 2004, Louisville philanthropist Owsley Brown Frazier elegantly refurbished the building and opened one of Louisville's newest state-of-the-art museums, The Frazier International History Museum—the only venue outside the United Kingdom to house historical artifacts from the prestigious Royal Armouries Collection.

Caufield and Shook Collection 145295 – 1936

Showcasing Frazier's personal collection of arms and historical artifacts, and in collaboration with the Royal Armouries Museum in Leeds, England, the Frazier International History Museum contains three floors of interactive exhibits and treasures ranging from arms belonging to England's monarchs to George Washington's flintlock rifle, to Teddy Roosevelt's "Big Stick," to a bow that belonged to Geronimo. The Frazier is the westernmost of Louisville's Main Street museums. Others along the West Main Street corridor include the Louisville Science Center, Hillerich & Bradsby's Louisville Slugger Museum and Factory, the Kentucky Art and Craft Museum and the Muhammad Ali Center.

LOUISVILLE SKYLINE

Skyline from the Second Street Bridge

In 1930, Louisville's wharf on the banks of the Ohio River was used for leisure activities but also served as a commercial hub. In this image, the *Hollywood Showboat* and the River Excursion Company's *America* were docked alongside the wharf boat later named the *Andrew Broaddus*, which is still moored there. On the left is the sign, "The Gateway to the South: Louisville," and it is possible to see landmarks like the Kentucky Hotel and even the L&N Building in the distance. The bridge from which this photo was taken—the Clark Memorial Bridge—had just been opened and tolls were being collected on the Indiana side of the bridge to pay off the enormous capital investment.

Caufield and Shook Collection 111493 – 1930

Today the wharf, formerly known as the levee, is home to the *Belle of Louisville* and is a hub of activity during the Kentucky Derby Festival's annual Great Steamboat Race. The skyline of Louisville has changed dramatically over the years, with hotels and office buildings rising in a cluster between First and Ninth Streets. Latest additions to the downtown skyline include a renovated Galt House and the Muhammad Ali Center, which opened in 2005—an international education and cultural facility designed to honor and share the legacy and ideals of "The Greatest," who was born in Louisville. Future plans call for construction of a 61-story Museum Plaza tower and a riverfront arena, hotel and retail complex.

WATERFRONT / LOUISVILLE GAS AND ELECTRIC COMPANY

River Road between Second and Third Streets

In the post-Civil War era, the Louisville Board of Trade coined the motto, "The Gateway to the South: Louisville," to promote the flow of Louisville's manufactured goods to the former Confederate states via the Louisville & Nashville Railroad. This motto appeared in lights atop the Kentucky Electric Company's riverfront generating station after that company merged with three other local utilities in 1913 to form the Louisville Gas and Electric Company. The sign, photographed here in 1938, welcomed arrivals to Louisville until blackouts were imposed during World War II.

Caufield and Shook Collection 156379 – 1938

Today the building still stands, minus its massive smokestacks and with other visible modifications, including the removal of the riverfront railroad tracks and spur leading to the plant. It still serves as an auxiliary source of power for the city and receives a boost from a huge poster image of Louisville's living legend, Muhammad Ali. The Louisville Arena Authority, however, plans to remove the buildings to make way for the construction of a new 24,000-seat downtown arena, hotel and retail complex on the waterfront site, to be completed by 2009.

WATERFRONT / GALT HOUSE HOTEL

View from Third Street Ramp

Originally the only exit off the "Riverside Expressway" into the center city, this ramp off Interstate 64 deposited traffic at the intersection of Third Street and River Road. In this photograph, the early stages of waterfront development can be seen but most of the buildings and hotels are yet to be built. This exit would soon provide a convenient entrance to a new Galt House hotel. This Galt House would be the third to bear the name. Author Charles Dickens visited the first, which opened at Second and Main Streets in 1835 but burned down in 1865. A second Galt House, built a block east on Main in 1869, remained in business for 50 years.

Gavin Whitsett Collection 1979.31.03 – 1970

Interstate 64 now passes across the city's waterfront. Since its completion, the public and private sectors have managed to build around it and have now reclaimed the waterfront with the bold Waterfront Park, a permanent landing for *The Belle of Louisville*, office buildings, condominiums and hotels. With the completion of a new Galt House hotel in 1972 and the Galt House East hotel in 1985, Louisville builder Al J. Schneider secured a foothold on the banks of the Ohio River. The Galt House towers at Fourth and Main are now popular host sites for scores of conferences and conventions each year. Recent renovations include redecorated rooms, an expanded ballroom in the Galt House East, and a glass conservatory spanning Fourth Street to connect the towers.

WATERFRONT WHARF

Idlewild / Avalon / Belle of Louisville / Andrew Broaddus Wharf Boat

First as the ferry *Idlewild*, then as an excursion craft called the *Avalon*, Louisville's signature steamboat was once based at Fontaine Ferry Park in West Louisville. Until the 1937 flood, Louisvillians enjoyed river excursions to Rose Island, a peninsula on the Indiana shore. The boat carried day-trippers on cruises from 1914 until 1962, when Jefferson County Judge Marlow Cooke spent $34,000 to buy her at auction. Renamed the *Belle of Louisville*, she competed in her first Derby week race against Cincinnati's *Delta Queen* in 1963.

Caufield and Shook Collection 133150 – 1934

Although the United States Life Saving Service operated on inland waters beginning in 1848, the nation's first and only surviving inland lifesaving station was established at Louisville's waterfront in 1881. Replaced with a new structure in 1902, and serving as a base of operation for the U.S. Coast Guard when it was formed in 1915, the current structure dates to 1928. Rescuers stationed at Louisville succeeded in saving the lives of thousands of inland mariners and millions of dollars worth of cargo from the waters around the Falls of the Ohio.

R.G. Potter Collection 3311

The *Belle of Louisville* still races each year in the Great Steamboat Race, a lighthearted and often mischievous contest that has become a key event of the annual Kentucky Derby Festival. In 1989, the National Park Service designated the *Belle* a National Historic Landmark. At 90, the *Belle* is the oldest rear paddle-wheeler still operating on the Ohio and Mississippi River systems.

The former Coast Guard station which replaced Life Saving Station No. 10 in 1928 now is named for Louisville Mayor Andrew Broaddus (1900-1972) who ordered an end to racial segregation of the city's public parks in 1955. Designated a National Historic Landmark in 1989, the *Andrew Broaddus* serves as a wharf boat and office for the *Belle of Louisville*.

WATERFRONT

Waterfront Park

For much of the city's history, Louisville's waterfront was dedicated to industrial uses. Dredging and scrapyard operations dominated the banks of the Ohio River. In the late 1960s, Interstate 64—first known as the "Riverside Expressway"—was constructed to connect other interstates in the area and across the country.

Gavin Whitsett Collection 1979.31.05 – 1970

In 1986, the Louisville Waterfront Development Corporation was created to partner with the City of Louisville, Jefferson County, and the Commonwealth of Kentucky in reclaiming Louisville's waterfront for civic purposes. The completion in 1999 of Waterfront Park and its centerpiece, The Great Lawn, was the first step toward the creation of new parks and public spaces, linking the entire border of the city to the river that gave it birth.

WATERFRONT

The Riverwalk

Finding the Falls of the Ohio to be an advantageous stopping point, settlers began a community on the south bank of the Ohio in 1779. Louisville was officially declared a town a year later, and for well over a century grew rapidly with the trade on the river. In the late 1980s an ambitious project began to reconnect Louisville with its roots as a river-dependent community. Louisville Mayor Jerry Abramson led efforts to acquire land on Louisville's waterfront so the rust piles, sand depots and oil storage tanks that lined the Ohio River could be transformed into green spaces and playgrounds.

Gavin Whitsett Collection 1979.31.28 – 1970

A dominant feature of Louisville's new Waterfront Park is the Riverwalk, an eight-mile-long pathway that links Chickasaw Park in the west to Carrie Gaulbert Cox Park in the east, with only a few gaps in between. The popular new pathway even runs along the Louisville and Portland Canal. Sidewalk information markers allow pedestrians, bicyclists and roller blade enthusiasts to exercise while learning about 19th-century life on the banks of the Ohio River.

In 2005, Mayor Abramson created a bold new initiative called City of Parks. The City and its Metro Parks Department invited groups like 21st Century Parks, the Olmsted Parks Conservatory, Future Fund and the Trust for Public Land to join them in an effort to surround Louisville Metro with an interconnected system of parks. With strong leadership being provided by civic leader David Jones and significant public support, plans are currently underway to acquire land to develop a 100-mile trail around Louisville Metro's perimeter and to improve the city's historic park system.

WATERFRONT

The Great Lawn

Before the Waterfront Development Corporation was created in 1986, Louisville's waterfront was cut off from the city and was filled with sand, gravel and scrap metal companies, warehouses, rail lines and barge facilities.

Caufield and Shook Collection 74515 – 1926

Twenty years later, the Waterfront Development Corporation—led by its executive director, David Karem—has developed 72 acres along Louisville's waterfront into award-winning parkland. The final 13 acres are now under construction, and hundreds of millions of dollars have been invested in the surrounding neighborhood. Waterfront Park now hosts over 100 events and welcomes over 1.25 million visitors each year. The Fifth Third Waterfront Independence Festival on the Park's Great Lawn, shown above, is one of the most popular Fourth of July celebrations in the community, featuring family activities, a free concert by a national artist and fireworks after dark.

Photograph courtesy of the Waterfront Development Corporation

FOURTH STREET LIVE!

Fourth Street, between Liberty Street and Muhammad Ali Boulevard

For over a century Fourth Street flourished as the city's premier retail center. As the suburban drain on the retail businesses in the inner city forced more and more stores to either relocate or close, city planners tried to imitate the suburban shopping experience by creating the River City Mall in 1970. Billed as a three-block-long, $1.5 million "people place," the concept of a River City Mall closed Fourth Street to automobile traffic so that shoppers could stroll in a park-like setting. The second generation of Fourth Street revitalization occurred with the 1982 opening of the Louisville Galleria, which placed shops and businesses inside a glass enclosure. Fourth Street remained closed to vehicular traffic except for trolleys, which were introduced in the 1980s as free transportation to move people around the inner-city core.

Caufield and Shook Collection 167356 – 1939

In 2001, the City of Louisville partnered with the Cordish Company of Baltimore, Maryland to create Fourth Street Live! — an exciting entertainment venue that re-opened Fourth Street to vehicular traffic and re-established the vitality of the Fourth Street corridor. Louisville residents and visitors again are "cruising Fourth Street" for the first time in decades.

The tall glass tower in the rear of the photograph above is the Meidinger Tower, a professional office building on the northwest corner of Fourth Street and Muhammad Ali Boulevard. Its twin tower, across from Borders Books on the southeast corner of Fourth and Liberty Streets, also houses professional offices, including the Louisville headquarters of Fifth Third Bank, a regular sponsor of concerts and events at Fourth Street Live!

THE KAUFMAN-STRAUS BUILDING / FOURTH STREET LIVE!

Fourth Street, between Liberty Street and Muhammad Ali Boulevard

The Kaufman-Straus Building, built on the site of the Louisville Polytechnic Society, was completed in 1903. Kaufman's Department Store (above, looking north on Fourth Street) occupied the lower floors until 1925, then claimed the entire building until 1971. By the 1960s, however, suburban malls and shopping centers drained business from the once-vibrant Fourth Street corridor. Not only were the suburban sites, with their free parking lots, closer to the post-war residences of Jefferson County, people considered shopping at the mall stores to be easier and more casual. Today there are still vestiges of the culture that dictated one be "dressed up" to "go downtown."

Chamber of Commerce Collection 1982.15.131 – circa 1950s

The downtown revitalization efforts of recent decades have incorporated the six-story Kaufman-Straus Building (above, looking south on Fourth Street). First enclosed under a glass roof for a 1980s architectural experiment called the Louisville Galleria, the building now anchors the east side of Fourth Street Live! and houses professional offices.

LG&E Collection 1990.11.108

KENTUCKY ELECTRIC COMPANY BUILDING / HSA BROADBAND BUILDING

600 Block of South Fourth Street, East Side

In 1912, the Kentucky Electric Company opened a new building at 619 South Fourth Street, but moved after only one year when the company was absorbed by the newly-formed Louisville Gas and Electric Company. Hubbuch Brothers and Wellendorff, shown in the photograph above, opened a carpet and home furnishings business in the building in 1919 and, in the 1940s, the building was occupied by Kunz's Delicatessen.

Caufield and Shook Collection 28739 - 1919

Abandoned amid the temporary decline of Fourth Street during the 1980s, the building achieved new life in 1997 when Louisville's Public Radio Partnership, formed by a unique collaboration of two radio stations previously operated by the Louisville Free Public Library and one owned by the University of Louisville, purchased the structure. Since 2000, the rehabilitated building has been known as the HSA Broadband Building. Although it has been transformed into a state-of-the-art space for broadcast, production and studio performance, the building is listed on the National Register of Historic Places.

THE SEELBACH HOTEL

Intersection of Fourth Street and Muhammad Ali Boulevard (formerly Walnut Street)

Louis Seelbach, a Bavarian immigrant, opened the first Seelbach Bar and Grill at Tenth and Main Streets in 1874. He later moved the establishment to Sixth and Main Streets and, with his brother Otto, opened a hotel above the Bar and Grill in 1886. The Seelbach became a popular, European-style hotel, but the brothers dreamed of opening a first-class, elegant hotel at the city's downtown center. In 1905, a new Seelbach Hotel was completed at Fourth and Muhammad Ali Boulevard (formerly known as Walnut Street). The sumptuous building was designed in the grand European style, outfitted with bronzes from France, original art murals, and Turkish and Persian rugs. It included a private dining room for men as well as a "Ladies Parlour." F. Scott Fitzgerald and gangster Al Capone were among many famous guests who stayed at the Seelbach. After it changed ownership several times, the hotel closed in 1975, as business moved away from the downtown area to the suburbs.

Royal Photo Studio Collection 10368.02 – 1948

The Seelbach Hotel, restored to its former prominence by actor and developer Roger Davis and construction company owner Gil Whittenberg, reopened in 1982. Today the hotel is a member of the Hilton family of hotels and holds a four-star, four-diamond-rated status. Its flagship restaurant, the Oakroom, was inducted into the Fine Dining Hall of Fame in 2001. The Old Seelbach Bar complements Louisville's newest entertainment complex, Fourth Street Live!

LOEW'S / UNITED ARTISTS STATE THEATRE / THE PALACE THEATRE

600 Block of South Fourth Street

Loew's/United Artists State Theatre opened September 1, 1928. This movie house was the Louisville location for all first-run Hollywood releases until suburban multiplexes and drive-ins scattered the once-faithful audiences. Over an 80-year history, four renovations have preserved the Spanish Baroque interior, while allowing the theater to adapt to changing cinematic technology. In the 1960s, a second movie theater called the Penthouse was located in the Loew's balcony.

Caufield and Shook Collection 121060 – 1931

Royal Photo Studio Collection 5196.07 – 1940

Having survived the wrecking ball on several occasions, the historic building re-opened its doors in 1994 as the Louisville Palace Theatre and is a glittering jewel along the revitalized Fourth Street corridor. The theater's restored interior still represents the night sky, complete with twinkling stars, and once again provides a hospitable venue for concerts, movies and special events of all kinds.

THEATER SQUARE

600 Block of South Fourth Street

Royal Photo Studio Collection 1038517 – 1948.

Packed with movie theaters like the Ohio, the Kentucky, and the Rialto, the 600 block of South Fourth Street stood as Louisville's Theater Row. In 1948, Louisvillians had bounced back from the war and were dressing up to visit downtown for shopping and movies. The Kentucky Theater (above left) opened in 1921 but underwent renovations, including the addition of a balcony, to accommodate tastes and increased demand from post-World War II audiences. Decades later, the Kentucky Theater survived the threat of demolition and, following another renovation, became home to the Kentucky Theater Project. At one point, the "Kentucky Show," a welcome to Louisville documentary, was shown in the old Kentucky Theater. While still occasionally providing a stage for emerging performers from the region, the Kentucky Theater today is best known as the venue of the public radio program "Kentucky Home Front." The Ohio Theater anchored the southern end of Fourth Street near the Brown Hotel. Its sign still stands today, on the east side of Fourth Street, while downtown Louisville's skyline has changed dramatically.

Caufield and Shook Collection 297143 – 1957

Caufield and Shook Collection 5847 – 1912

SOUTHERN BELL / SOUTH CENTRAL BELL / BELLSOUTH

521 West Chestnut Street / 601 West Chestnut Street

Telephone service came to Louisville in 1879, when local businessman James B. Speed had a telephone line installed to connect his office on Main Street with his cement mill in Portland. Service grew rapidly from there, with the 1880 Louisville telephone directory listing 600 local telephone subscribers. In 1884, the first building in the world constructed solely to house a telephone exchange was built at 424 West Jefferson Street in Louisville. The ensuing decades saw competition and growth as the Ohio Valley Telephone Company, the Cumberland Telephone and Telegraph Company, and the Louisville Home Telephone Company pushed the total number of telephones in Louisville to 53,000. In 1925, the Southern Bell Telephone and Telegraph system consolidated all the companies into a modern network. Southern Bell opened a 10-story headquarters on Chestnut Street in 1930.

R.G. Potter Collection 6928 – 1930

In the earliest days, local telephone linemen and installers used horse-drawn wagons for their service appointments and facilities construction, as shown in this Louisville Home Telephone Company employee photo circa 1900.

Photo courtesy of BellSouth

Shifts in the telecommunications industry in the 1970s to fully electronic switching systems and digital information storage caused South Central Bell to seek new, expanded space for its Kentucky state administrative offices and electronic data centers. In 1978, the company constructed and moved into a new headquarters building at 601 West Chestnut Street. The original South Central Bell building across Sixth Street now houses AT&T.

Photo courtesy of BellSouth

Today, BellSouth employees like those pictured here use modern service vans and state-of-the-art equipment to provide high-speed Internet, data and voice services to many thousands of homes and businesses throughout the Louisville Metro area.

Photo courtesy of BellSouth

Photo courtesy of Scott Stortz

PRESBYTERIAN SEMINARY / JEFFERSON COMMUNITY AND TECHNICAL COLLEGE

109 East Broadway

For much of the 19th and well into the 20th centuries, Gothic and Renaissance Revival-style buildings (including the first structures of the Southern Baptist Seminary and St. Xavier High School) and a number of private residences lined Broadway. Only a handful remain today, including this downtown campus of Jefferson Community and Technical College. Built in 1902 as the Louisville Presbyterian Theological Seminary, the ornate quadrangle draws inspiration from the colleges of Oxford University. The Louisville Presbyterian Theological Seminary moved to a new campus in the city's east end in 1963. Its presence in Louisville helped Presbyterian Church (USA) make the decision to bring its national headquarters to the community in 1987.

Caufield and Shook Collection 161222 – 1938

Jefferson Community and Technical College (above), which opened on Broadway in 1968, now has over 13,000 students, four additional campuses across Louisville Metro, and is the largest school in the Kentucky Community and Technical College System. In October 2005, Jefferson Community and Technical College announced efforts to reclaim original murals and drawings that were painted over during renovation in the 1960s.

YMCA / ST. FRANCIS HIGH SCHOOL

Northeast Corner of Third Street and Broadway

The YMCA building on the corner of Third Street and Broadway was known as the "Central Y." The seven-story structure was completed in 1913 and served as the main YMCA in Louisville for over six decades. This photograph shows the height of the famous 1937 Ohio River flood, which crested well beyond Broadway, covering two-thirds of the City of Louisville. Boats plied the waters on Broadway as rescue teams ferried people to higher ground.

R.G. Potter Collection 520 – 1937

The YMCA building still anchors the northeast corner of Third and Broadway. In the 1980s, the "Old Y" was threatened with demolition but was rescued on the eve of its destruction by a team of local investors, led by William J. Receveur, Jr., who renovated the building to accommodate the classroom needs of St. Francis High School. The building was later sold to St. Francis and today includes condominiums and offices, in addition to the school. The YMCA moved to its new quarters at 555 South Second Street in 1976.

THE BROWN HOTEL

Northeast Corner of Fourth Street

This photo of Broadway at Fourth Street taken at the turn of the last century reflects the residential nature of the street. For decades, The northeast corner of Broadway was an attractive address for homes and small businesses like Solger's ice cream parlor, shown here. In this 1920 photo, a traffic officer with his stop-and-go sign controls traffic at the intersection while people wait for the Broadway trolley. People were once able to board the trolley from an island in the middle of the street. Solger's gave way in 1923 to the Brown Hotel.

R.G. Potter Collection 4955 – circa 1920

The same corner is now the site of the Brown Hotel. Built by James Graham Brown in honor of his brother Martin, the Brown Hotel first welcomed guests to its Crystal Ballroom and English Grill in 1923. Upon James Graham Brown's death in 1969, his foundation sold the hotel to the Louisville Board of Education, which used the historic property as administrative offices from 1971 until the merger of the Louisville and Jefferson County Public Schools. Restored to its former glory in a 1985 renovation, the hotel now operates as the Camberley Brown Hotel and once more serves the famous "Hot Brown" invented by Chef Fred K. Schmidt in 1926. The English Grill, home of acclaimed Chef Joe Castro, is repeatedly honored as Louisville's best restaurant and has been designated a AAA Four-Diamond restaurant.

BROADWAY / BROWN HOTEL / HEYBURN BUILDING / KINDRED HEALTHCARE / BROWN BROTHERS CADILLAC

Broadway at Fifth Street, looking East

The intersection of Fourth and Broadway in the 1930s, 1940s and 1950s was a busy place. Called the "magic corner," it was arguably Louisville's city center before the "back to the waterfront" developments of the 1960s, 1970s and 1980s. On the north side (the left side of the photo above) stood the Commonwealth Life Insurance building (shown here before the addition of some 20 stories) and the Brown Hotel. On the south corners were the Heyburn Building, built in a classical office style and completed in 1929, and the Warren Memorial Presbyterian Church.

R.G. Potter Collection 3349 – circa 1940

Today the intersection of Fourth and Broadway anchors the reinvigorated Fourth Street corridor. The Brown Hotel and the Heyburn Building are still standing and each has been restored and renovated. The northwest corner, where the former Commonwealth Life Insurance Building stood, is now a gated green space. The six-story brick building just west of the green space is the headquarters of Kindred Healthcare, a national healthcare services company and Fortune 500 company. The southwest corner has been occupied by the Brown Brothers Cadillac dealership for decades.

THE COURIER-JOURNAL

525 West Broadway

Since 1868, *The Courier-Journal* has served as the region's principal print news source. The newspaper's distinguished legacy of fine journalism boasts nine Pulitzer Prizes. Its seven-story building on the northeast corner of Sixth and Broadway, built at the end of World War II, drew inspiration from Art Deco style and provided a handsome headquarters for the Bingham family newspaper enterprises—*The Courier Journal* and, until 1987, *The Louisville Times*. WHAS Radio and TV were also once housed in the *Courier-Journal* building.

Caufield and Shook Collection 10753 – 1948

The view looking west down Broadway has now changed. *The Courier-Journal* has created new parking spaces on the east side of the building. The Gannett Company, Inc., which purchased *The Courier-Journal* in 1986, spent $85 million on a 135,000-square-foot expansion in 2004, adding additional press and color capacity to the newspaper.

UNION STATION / TRANSIT AUTHORITY OF RIVER CITY (TARC) HEADQUARTERS

Broadway at Tenth Street

Louisville's principal train station from its opening in 1891 until train service ceased in 1976, Union Station at Tenth and Broadway served the Louisville-based Louisville & Nashville (L&N) Railroad and, later, Amtrak. For nearly a century, except for 12 days when high water forced closing during the 1937 flood, Union Station was the point of arrival for visitors, immigrants, soldiers (traveling to and from nearby Ft. Knox), and the hordes coming to Louisville each May to attend the Kentucky Derby. Union Station's exterior has changed little from the original design by F.W. Mowbray.

Terhune collection 87.70.04 – 1907

The interior of Union Station is dominated by a large, barrel-vaulted ceiling. The north wall features a massive stained-glass rose window. An ornate wrought-iron railing encloses the second floor balcony space.

When passenger rail service virtually disappeared in the late 1970s, the L&N Railroad sold Union Station to the city's bus service company, the Transit Authority of River City (TARC).

Today the historic structure continues as a transportation center. A renovation completed in 1980 preserved Union Station's unique architecture, and it now provides a public reception space for TARC.

Caufield and Shook Collection 192460 – 1943

OLD LOUISVILLE WATER COMPANY SITE
Third Street between Liberty Street and Muhammad Ali Boulevard

Around 1900, the Louisville Water Company launched a public campaign to convince citizens that their own private well water could be laden with toxic bacteria. The effort attracted many new city water customers. Louisville's first water company and pumping station still stands at River Road and Zorn Avenue, but the Ohio River's recurring floods forced the functions of the facility inland in 1882, and into a new headquarters at 435 South Third Street (above) in 1910.

Caufield and Shook Collection 144004 – 1936

Today, the old Louisville Water Company building, only slightly modified and now surrounded by large trees, survives as a Louisville Metro Police Department substation.

In 1998, the Louisville Water Company moved its headquarters toward Broadway into a new structure at 550 South Third Street. Designed by the Louis and Henry Group, the new Louisville Water Company building and its adjoining parking structure include architectural allusions to the flow of water and the city's historic pumping station, now known as the Water Tower, on the Ohio River. The Louisville Water Company, proud of its 150-year record of pure water, distributes its special "Pure Tap" individual drinking bottles at community events.

Photo courtesy of Scott Stortz

THE LOUISVILLE FREE PUBLIC LIBRARY

301 York Street

Between 1886 and 1921, philanthropist Andrew Carnegie offered cities across the country financial assistance to build over 1,700 libraries. Cities signed an agreement to provide land and long-term maintenance for the libraries and, in turn, Carnegie provided funds for the "bricks and mortar." Louisville obtained funding for and constructed nine Carnegie libraries and all are now listed in the National Register of Historic Places. The main branch of the Louisville Free Public Library at Fourth and York Streets was constructed in 1908. Designed by Pilcher and Tachau, a New York firm chosen after an invitational competition, it is considered to be an outstanding example of Beaux-Arts Classicism. In the 1950s, the Louisville Free Public Library system offered bookmobiles and University of Louisville courses through its Neighborhood College program. It also established public radio stations for classical music and jazz – WFPL and WFPK – which are now part of Louisville's Public Radio Partnership.

Civic pride in the Louisville Free Public Library building made it an attractive backdrop for advertisements, especially those involving automobiles. The above photograph, taken for an advertisement for dealership Bonnie, Smith & Epperson, features a 1920 Winton hearse, complete with gas lights. Winton, which began manufacturing cars in 1897, was America's first model of horseless carriage.

Caufield and Shook Collection 34007 – 1920

Still "free to all," the Louisville Free Public Library now offers access to computers and databases, books-on-tape and other state-of-the art researching resources, in addition to books, periodicals and programs for the community. City of Louisville funding is augmented by grants and other monies raised privately through the Friends of the Library. A community-wide book sale the group hosts is a popular annual event. An expansion to the north has increased space at the main branch of the Louisville Free Public Library at Fourth and York Streets. Sixteen branches are located across Louisville Metro, with plans underway to construct three regional libraries.

Photo courtesy of Scott Stortz

COLUMBIA AUDITORIUM / SPALDING UNIVERSITY

824 South Fourth Street

This Classical Revival building was designed by Thomas Nolan and built in 1925. The Columbia Auditorium became the original home of the Kentucky Opera in 1952, despite the fact that it had no orchestra pit. The Opera moved its productions to the Brown Theatre on Broadway in 1963. The Columbia Auditorium also played a prominent role in the life of Louisville-born boxer Cassius Clay, later known as Muhammad Ali. In 1954, at the age of 12, Ali's bicycle was stolen while he was attending an event at the Columbia Auditorium. Ali approached a police officer who was teaching a class in the building to tell him about his loss, and expressed a desire to seek revenge for the theft. Officer Joe Martin convinced the young Cassius Clay to take up boxing instead at a local gymnasium, and the rest, of course, is history.

Caufield and Shook Collection – 1948

The building has been in continuous use from its inception and today is part of Spalding University's downtown campus. Spalding University was the first four-year college for women in Kentucky and traces its history back to Nazareth College, founded by the Sisters of Charity of Nazareth in 1920. It now bears the name of Catherine Spalding who established the historic order in 1813. It has been co-educational since 1973 and is known for its innovative approach to intensive course scheduling.

TEMPLE ADATH ISRAEL / GREATER BETHEL TEMPLE APOSTOLIC CHURCH

834 South Third Street

Early in the 20th century, Temple Adath Israel at Sixth and Broadway literally began to collapse, so the congregation found a new location on Third Street, held a design competition, then selected the firm of McDonald and Sheblessy. The impressive neo-classical design of the building was similar to mainstream churches of the time, including the First Christian Church one block west on Fourth Street. The building served the Adath Israel congregation from 1906 until 1977.

Caufield and Shook Collection 6988 – 1915

In 1976, with merger talks underway between Adath Israel and Brith Sholom, the Adath Israel membership voted to move from this structure and build a new synagogue on land it owned on the corner of Brownsboro Road and Lime Kiln Lane, closer to the congregation's members in the eastern suburbs. By 1979, the two congregations merged and re-named their new congregation "The Temple." Adath Israel sold the building to the Greater Bethel Temple Apostolic Church. Today the building's exterior is largely unchanged, and the interfaith message above the colossal columns is also unchanged: "Mine House Shall Be An House of Prayer for All People."

CATHEDRAL OF THE ASSUMPTION

443 South Fifth Street

St. Louis, the city's first Roman Catholic Church, was established in 1811 at Tenth and Main Streets but moved to South Fifth Street in 1830. When the diocesan seat was moved from Bardstown to Louisville In 1841, St. Louis served as the first cathedral. In 1849, construction began on a new building, which opened as the Cathedral of the Assumption in 1852. The bodies of two bishops and one priest are entombed underneath the Cathedral's altar.

Caufield and Shook Collection 270047 – 1910.

A restoration of the Cathedral of the Assumption in 1985 by the Cathedral Heritage Foundation, spearheaded by Christina Lee Brown, transformed the interior of the historic structure. The exterior was also refurbished and the steeple removed, restored and replaced. The Cathedral Heritage Foundation created and now hosts a prestigious interfaith event each year at the Cathedral called The Festival of Faiths.

Vintage postcard image courtesy of Mike Maloney - circa 1930s

CENTRAL PARK

Fourth to Sixth Street / Park Avenue to Magnolia Street

Central Park was developed after Louisville's Southern Exposition closed in 1887. It was one of Louisville's Olmsted Parks, located on land between Fourth and Sixth Streets originally occupied by the duPont family's estate. Citizens were lured to Central Park—which in fact was central to nothing—because it was purposely located on duPont's trolley line. The park's historic colonnade dates back to 1905. In the early days, an indoor fitness center and swimming pool were located in the building where a district police substation is now.

Caufield and Shook Collection 50442 – circa 1915

The colonnade still exists, but Central Park itself has changed. A portion of the park's 17 acres now is the location of a Louisville Metro police substation. The park also hosts the Kentucky Shakespeare Festival's "Shakespeare in Central Park" each summer at the C. Douglas Ramey Amphitheatre.

ST. JAMES COURT / BELGRAVIA COURT

Fourth to Sixth Street / Magnolia to Hill Streets

St. James Court and the intersecting Belgravia Court were built on the site of the 1883-1887 Southern Exposition. Belgravia Court was named after a fashionable London district. St. James Court refers to the seat of the British monarchy. The Courts were built to imitate an upper-class English residential area, complete with an esplanade, a fountain and an Episcopal church located on the northeast corner. An 1890 deed restriction required all homes to have either brick or stone construction. The one wooden house in the neighborhood, 1412 St. James Court, was built as a playhouse for the children of the duPont family and was moved to its present site after the duPonts sold their land to the City to become Central Park.

Caufield and Shook Collection 51031 – 1923

Today St. James Court and Belgravia Court are still prestigious addresses. Nearly all of the large, stylish homes have been preserved and lovingly renovated. The area remains quiet and gentrified, except for the first weekend in October when the neighborhood hosts the St. James Court Art Fair. The Court has been the site of the annual art show since 1957. The St. James Court Art Fair is celebrated as one of the largest and best in the United States. Proceeds fund preservation projects and amenities for the courts and the surrounding neighborhoods.

JEWISH HOSPITAL / JEWISH HOSPITAL & ST. MARY'S HEALTHCARE

Chestnut at Brook Street

The anchor of the Jewish Hospital Health Network, Jewish Hospital was incorporated in 1903 and opened as a 32-bed hospital in 1905. The first Jewish Hospital building, on the southwest corner of Kentucky and Brook Streets, is now an apartment building. Originally established to provide care for Jewish immigrants, Jewish Hospital broadened its outreach and responded to the community's post-World War II efforts to gather health care resources into a medical campus near downtown Louisville.

Caufield and Shook Collection 15900 – 1956

Since moving into a new building on Chestnut Street in 1955, Jewish Hospital HealthCare Services has opened additional facilities downtown and in the Louisville Metro suburbs. Jewish Hospital & St. Mary's Healthcare, as the healthcare system is now known, is an internationally-recognized center for innovative transplant procedures, including the world's first hand transplant and the world's first completely self-contained artificial heart transplant.

OLD LOUISVILLE PUBLIC HOSPITAL / ABELL ADMINISTRATON BUILDING

East Chestnut Street, Between Preston and Floyd Streets

The University of Louisville Medical School assumed responsibility for the Louisville City Hospital soon after a new structure opened on East Chestnut Street in 1914. In 1948, Louisville urban planners recommended that the area's hospitals concentrate in one area, near the University of Louisville and its Louisville General Hospital.

Caufield and Shook Collection 123149 – 1932

This historic Louisville General Hospital Building now serves as the Abell Administration Building for the University of Louisville's Health Sciences Center and is at the center of the Louisville Medical Center. This unique organization, dedicated to leading-edge research, diagnosis and treatment, is composed of the University of Louisville Health Sciences Center, University of Louisville Hospital, Jewish Hospital, Norton Hospital, Kosair Children's Hospital, the James Graham Brown Cancer Center and nearly 200 other partners and serves more than half a million patients each year. A strong focus on research within the University of Louisville Health Sciences Center has resulted in a dramatic increase in federal research funding—in fact, the largest percentage growth in National Institutes of Health funding of any university—and development of a new Life Sciences Research Park.

UNIVERSITY OF LOUISVILLE HOSPITAL

Jackson Street Between Chestnut Street and Muhammad Ali Boulevard

In 1944, the area around Jackson and Madison Streets was largely residential, with a few small businesses punctuating each block. In this view members of Louisville Kiwanis Club are digging a wading pool for a community park. The smokestack of Frank Fehr Brewing Company on Fehr Avenue rises in the background.

Caufield and Shook Collection 195571 – 1944

Although the University of Louisville had operated Louisville General Hospital on Chestnut Street since soon after it opened in 1914, the university's concern for patient care, as well as its research and teaching missions, outgrew the facility on Chestnut Street. In 1983, in partnership with Humana, Inc., the University opened a state-of-the-art hospital on South Jackson Street, establishing a new eastern border for Louisville's downtown medical center. In 1996, the hospital partnered with Jewish Hospital HealthCare Services and Norton Healthcare to form University Medical Center Inc. and assumed operation of University Hospital. Since 1999, the partnership also has included the James Graham Brown Cancer Center and University Physicians Group.

METHODIST EVANGELICAL HOSPITAL / NORTON HEALTHCARE PAVILION

Preston at Gray Street

This block of Preston at Gray Street, running south to Broadway, housed a succession of businesses over the years, from barbers to greengrocers to used furniture sales outlets. Only Louisville Curtain and Blanket Laundry, closer to Broadway, remained in continuous operation. After this 1963 photograph was taken, these buildings were razed to allow expansion of Methodist Evangelical Hospital, which had opened three years earlier.

Royal Photo Studio Collection 18177.03 – 1963

Norton Memorial Infirmary, which had operated at Third and Oak Streets since 1886, merged with Children's Hospital in 1969 and joined the city's developing medical complex. Norton Hospital opened in a new building in its current location at 200 East Chestnut Street in 1973. Methodist Evangelical Hospital, pictured here, opened in 1960. Methodist eventually merged with NKC Hospitals, Inc. (as Norton was known at the time) and the building was renamed the Alliant Medical Pavilion. Today the facility is known as the Norton Healthcare Pavilion and houses clinics and physician offices. Norton Healthcare is now Kentucky's largest health care provider, with five hospitals and seven immediate care centers in the area.

CLARKSDALE / LIBERTY GREEN

East Jefferson Street to Muhammad Ali Boulevard
Shelby to Jackson Streets

Clarksdale was the first public housing development built by the Housing Authority of Louisville under the Housing Act of 1937. Clarksdale covered six city blocks east of downtown and provided over 700 units of public housing.

Photos courtesy of Louisville Metro Housing Authority

In 2004, a collaborative effort by Louisville Metro Government, Louisville Metro Housing Authority and the U.S. Department of Housing and Urban Development began to replace the 67-year-old structures with new apartments, town homes and condominiums. Liberty Green, which establishes a new mixed-income community in Louisville's urban center, is being constructed in two phases and is scheduled to be completed in 2009.

BROWN-FORMAN CORPORATION

850 Dixie Highway

Founded in 1870, Brown-Forman pioneered the practice of selling its Old Forester Bourbon in sealed bottles instead of in barrels that subjected the product to the risk of dilution by unscrupulous vendors. During the era of Prohibition, Brown-Forman secured one of 10 national licenses to sell its Kentucky bourbon for medicinal purposes. Brown-Forman celebrated its first century in 1970 by publishing a book—*There's Nothing Better in the Market*—about the company's history and by renovating a historic bourbon warehouse on Dixie Highway into corporate offices.

R.G. Potter Collection 3925 – circa 1935

Over the following decades, the company diversified to offer a range of wines and spirits, including the world's best-selling whiskey, Jack Daniel's. One of its oldest and most famous offerings, Old Forester Bourbon, is still advertised on a water tower atop the headquarters. That distinctive water tower is a landmark for the neighborhood, which has been revitalized with support from Brown-Forman.

MCALPINE LOCKS AND DAM

2700 Block of Northwestern Parkway

The locks located off North 27th Street (in the Portland neighborhood, at mile point 606.8 of the Ohio River), were completed in 1830 to allow shipping traffic to bypass the Falls of the Ohio River. Originally constructed of wood and consisting of three stair-step chambers, the locks were built on the Louisville side of the river in the Louisville-Portland Canal and were the first major engineering project on the Ohio River. The first modern locks (above) were completed in 1921. A hydroelectric dam was added in 1925-1927. Finally, in 1961, a new main chamber measuring 110 feet by 1200 feet was completed and named the McAlpine Locks to honor William McAlpine, a former Louisville District Engineer.

Caufield and Shook Collection 37367 – 1921

Today the McAlpine Locks handle 55 million tons of commodities per year, with coal comprising about 38 percent of the total. More tonnage, in fact, moves through these locks annually than moves through the Panama Canal. In October 2003, the McAlpine Locks and Dam were designated together as a Historic Civil Engineering Landmark by the American Society of Civil Engineers. The locks are currently undergoing a 10-year, $278 million expansion, including construction of a parallel lock, which will be completed in 2008.

U.S. MARINE HOSPITAL

2200 Block of Northwestern Parkway

Inspired by the need to provide health care to boatmen working on the Ohio River during the steamboat era, Congress authorized the creation of seven inland federal hospitals. Designed by Robert Mills, the architect of the Washington Monument and other significant federal buildings, the Louisville hospital opened for patients in 1852. The hospital served boatmen, who paid 20 cents a month in the nation's first pre-paid health insurance program. In later years, the Marine Hospital served Civil War soldiers, Coast Guard personnel, and veterans of the Spanish-American War and World War I. The hospital served patients until 1933 when the Works Progress Administration built today's Family Health Center. The U.S. Marine Hospital is the sole surviving example of Robert Mills' original seven facilities.

Photo courtesy of The National Archives

Because of its significance to public health and maritime commerce, the U.S. Marine Hospital was designated a National Historic Landmark in 1997. The building was declared one of America's 11 Most Endangered Places by the National Trust for Historic Preservation in 2003, which helped stimulate support to restore and renew the majestic old hospital. After raising $2.5 million and being awarded Save America's Treasures status in 2003, the U.S. Marine Hospital Foundation began exterior restoration in 2005. The exterior restoration phase was completed in November 2006, with plans for the interior restoration and public use of the building currently under way.

WHITESIDE BAKERY

West Broadway at 14th Street

Louisville's "Broadway" was once named Prather Street. The Whiteside Bakery opened in 1908 on Broadway as one of the nation's most progressive commercial bakery operations. The plant was designed to benefit from its proximity to a spur of the Pennsylvania Railroad, which enabled the bakery to take advantage of ready access to raw materials.

Caufield and Shook Collection 97203 – 1928

Although a number of bakeries, most recently the Dixie Baking Company, occupied the building through the 1970s, today the handsome Mission-style building houses a used car and auto parts company.

PARK DUVALLE NEIGHBORHOOD

Shawnee Expressway / Cypress Street / Algonquin Parkway

Park DuValle is the name given to the neighborhood in West Louisville roughly bounded by the Shawnee Expressway, Cypress Street and Algonquin Parkway. Lucie N. DuValle, an African-American educator, was the first female principal in the Louisville public school system. Although the neighborhood's existence can be traced to the so-called Little Africa, a community of African-Americans living here after the Civil War, the neighborhood was basically designed by urban renewal efforts in the 1950s, when it became Cotter and Lang housing projects.

Royal Photo Studio Collection 16421.13 – 1958

In the late 1960s, Dr. Harvey Sloane (who would become Louisville's mayor in 1973), obtained a major government grant and began to revive the Park DuValle neighborhood by starting the Park DuValle Community Health Center. Under the leadership of Mayor Jerry Abramson, and funded in large part by a Hope VI grant, the aging Cotter and Lang buildings were razed starting in the mid-1990s to make way for the construction of 1,200+ new homes and townhouses in the Park DuValle neighborhood.

SHAWNEE PARK

Shawnee Park, one of Louisville's three original Olmsted-designed parks, opened in 1892. The grass in the park was first "cut" by grazing sheep. Shawnee Park gained popularity with the arrival of a streetcar line in 1895 and the subsequent opening of the nearby Fontaine Ferry Amusement Park in 1905. The amusement park has been closed since 1975, but Shawnee Park continues to be a popular site for sports leagues, picnics, family reunions and a variety of special events, including concerts hosted at the historic band shell pictured above.

Caufield and Shook Collection 112393 – 1930

Frederick Law Olmsted, the renowned "Father of American Landscape Architecture," designed only five park systems in the country and many believe Louisville's was his finest and most scenic. The Olmsted Parks and Parkways, which weave through the city's neighborhoods, are often referred to as Louisville's "Emerald Necklace." Louisville works hard to restore, enhance and preserve its treasured Olmsted Parks and Parkways. In 2004, the city saved and renovated the band shell in Shawnee Park. Concerts and other events are once again held in this popular venue. Shawnee Park's golf course along the banks of the Ohio River in West Louisville now also serves as home to the BellSouth Youth Golf Academy.

OLD STATE FAIRGROUNDS / MERCHANT AND MANUFACTURERS BUILDING / WHAYNE SUPPLY COMPANY

1400 Cecil Avenue

When the Kentucky Board of Agriculture designated Louisville as the permanent site for the Kentucky State Fair early in the 20th century, the state acquired 150 acres in the southwest corner of the city at the end of Cecil Avenue, west of 38th Street and north of Gibson Lane. Visitors were impressed with what was, at that time, the largest livestock pavilion in the state. In 1921, the Merchants and Manufacturers Building opened in a structure larger than Madison Square Garden. In spite of these impressive facilities, however, the site began to show its age and became inadequate for the growing needs of the State Fair. In 1956, the fair moved to its current location at the Kentucky Fair and Exposition Center near the Louisville airport.

Caufield and Shook Collection 44550 – 1922

Today, the Spanish Renaissance-style building designed by Louisville architects Joseph & Joseph is largely unchanged from its original design. Whayne Supply Company, once on Main Street, now uses the site for its offices and warehouse space.

KENTUCKY FAIR AND EXPOSITION CENTER

900 Block of Phillips Lane

The first Kentucky State Fair was held in 1902 at Churchill Downs. A dedicated Kentucky state fairgrounds opened in West Louisville in 1906. The current Kentucky Fair and Exposition Center—located near the airport, west of Interstate 65 and north of Interstate 264—first welcomed crowds in 1956. One of the city's worst traffic jams occurred when the new fairgrounds opened. Initially ranging over 356 acres and costing $16 million, the complex has grown steadily since it was completed, and is now the nation's sixth-largest exposition facility. Freddy Farm Bureau, a giant talking puppet that can be seen near the center of this 1961 photo and in the photo on the opposite page, still welcomes fair-goers.

Caufield and Shook Collection B-1914-4 – 1961

The Kentucky Fair and Exposition Center attracts nearly three million visitors year-round to conventions, concerts, sporting events and exhibitions, including the Kentucky State Fair. Freedom Hall is home to University of Louisville basketball and the Louisville Fire Arena Football team. Six Flags Kentucky Kingdom amusement park is also located on the grounds. In 2006, the facility was renamed the Kentucky Exposition Center.

Photo courtesy of The Kentucky Fair and Exposition Center

J.B. SPEED ART MUSEUM

2035 South Third Street

The University of Louisville's Belknap Campus was only two years old when Hattie Bishop Speed funded the construction of an art museum on the university's west side. She named it the Speed Museum in honor of her deceased husband, John Breckinridge Speed. The museum opened in January, 1927, with no admission fee required. It was an instant hit with Louisvillians, who came by the hundreds of thousands to see the museum's collections.

Louisville Herald Post Collection 1994.18.0488 – 1930

Almost 80 years and several renovations later, the Neo-Classical Revival building is still Louisville's most distinguished museum destination, with an impressive permanent collection and gallery space for a prestigious list of first-class traveling exhibitions.

STANDIFORD FIELD / LOUISVILLE INTERNATIONAL AIRPORT

Standiford Field replaced Bowman Field as Louisville's commercial airline facility on November 15, 1947. The airport is situated on 1,200 acres once owned by Dr. Elisha David Standiford—a farmer, businessman and legislator for whom the airport is named. Dr. Standiford served as president of the L & N Railroad. Lee Terminal, shown above, opened in May, 1950. The $1 million, 42,000-square-foot facility boasted six gates, a 300-space parking lot, and an annual capacity of 150,000 passengers. It was named for Addison Lee, Jr., who had served as chairman of the Louisville Regional Airport Authority for 20 years. Standiford Field has continuously expanded since it opened.

Royal Photo Studio Collection 12957 – 1951

Between 1960 and 1970, passenger traffic at then-Standiford Field increased to a million passengers per year. In 1962, when this photograph was taken, passengers continued to use portable stairs to board and disembark from aircraft, walking across the aircraft apron to the terminal. Delta Air Lines—one of the oldest continually-operating airlines in Louisville—had its own concourse, built in 1970, which was the first in Louisville to offer into-plane boarding from the terminal.

Caufield and Shook Collection 2027 – 1

The airport's name was changed in 1995 to reflect changes in the airport's operations and vision for the future, particularly after UPS established its US international package hub in Louisville. Although Standiford Field is now formally known as the Louisville International Airport, airline bookings to Louisville are still designated to arrive at "SDF." The terminal's size and capacity has shown pronounced and continuous growth through the decades. In 2005, a $41 million terminal renovation was completed to expand facilities, upgrade service amenities, and give the airport a more modern ambience.

Delta Air Lines is one of seven passenger airline brands currently serving the Louisville market and continues as a predominant carrier in the city. Delta Air Lines originated the passenger hub system which has since been employed by other legacy carriers. Louisville passenger carriers employ a combination of mid-size and regional jets for more efficient service and frequency.

Photo courtesy of Scott Stortz

UPS GLOBAL AIR HUB – WORLDPORT

Louisville International Airport

Photo courtesy of Greater Louisville Inc.

As UPS expanded its air operation in late 1981-early 1982, the company purchased 20 Boeing 727-100 aircraft. Painted with a brown tail, the aircraft allowed UPS to reach 38 states by the end of 1982.

United Parcel Service (UPS), currently Louisville's largest employer with more than 20,000 full- and part-time employees in the Commonwealth, has been in an almost continuous mode of expansion since it stepped up its Louisville sorting operation in 1981. The following year, Louisville's small regional hub of about 100 employees became UPS's main air hub, employing nearly 1000 employees to sort packages for seven daily flights. By 1997, UPS had expanded into hundreds of international markets, employing 14,000 people to accommodate over 100 flights per day.

LOUISVILLE 158 THEN AND NOW

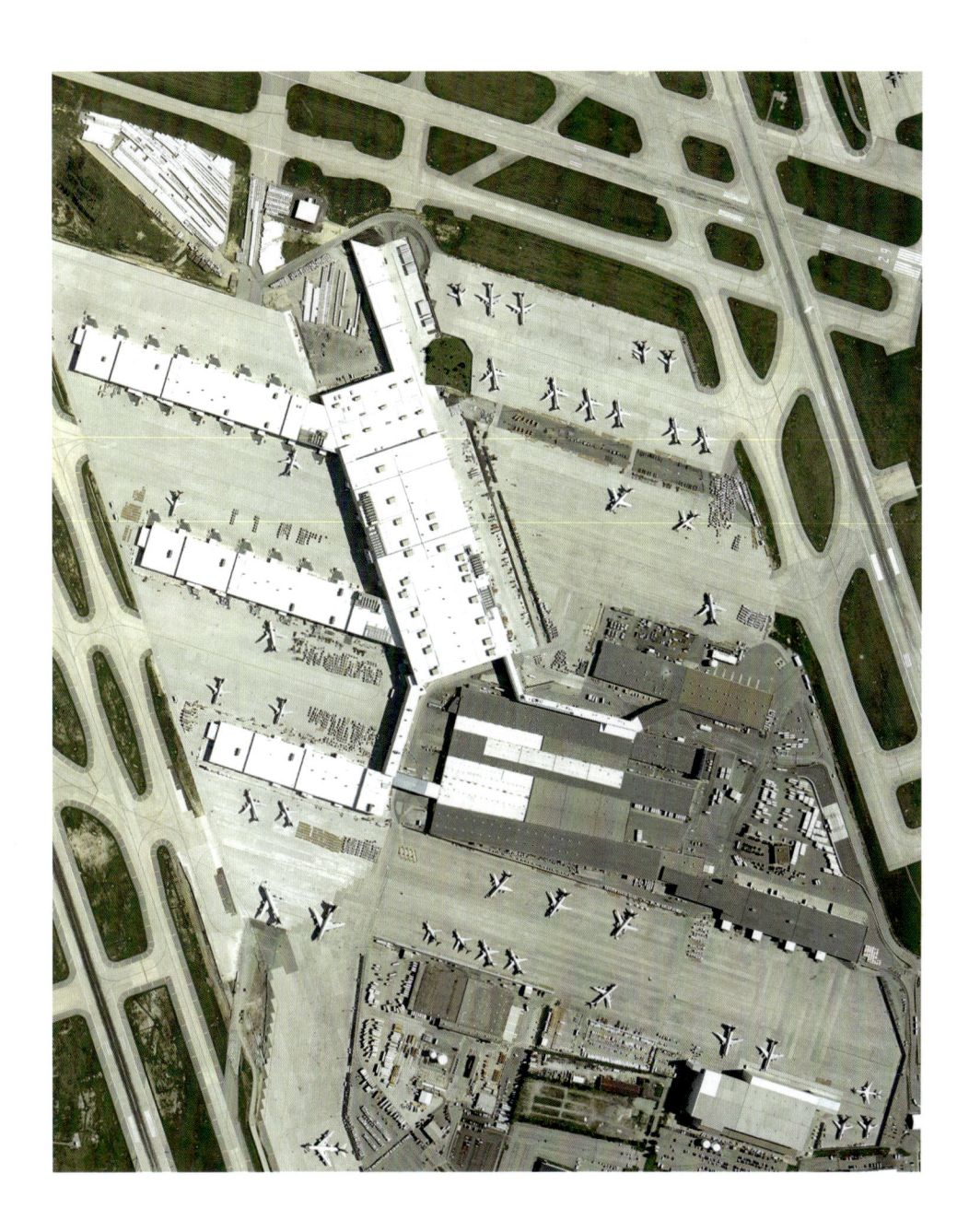

Now the eighth-largest airline in the world and serving over 200 countries worldwide, UPS is a global leader in delivery and logistics services and a regional leader in supporting community and charitable causes. The new brandmark and aircraft paint scheme reflect the significant broadening of capabilities that has occurred in recent years as the company has expanded across the globe and introduced a portfolio of new services.

In 1998, UPS announced a $700 million expansion of its operations at Standiford Field, re-named Louisville International Airport, including the addition of a new mega-sorting center and two parallel runways. In 2005, UPS announced plans to add a heavy airfreight hub to its facilities, and in 2006 announced a $1 billion expansion and the addition of over 5000 new jobs to its Louisville Worldport℠ by 2010. UPS processes about 14.8 million ground packages a day and about 1 million packages a day through its Worldport℠ facility.

Photos courtesy of UPS

CHURCHILL DOWNS

700 Block of Central Avenue

Churchill Downs is famous throughout the world as the home of the "fastest two minutes in sports," the Kentucky Derby. The Downs has provided a focus for thoroughbred racing since 1875 when Meriwether Lewis Clark, Jr. (grandson of William Clark, one of the leaders of the Lewis and Clark expedition, and great-nephew of George Rogers Clark, the founder of Louisville) established the Louisville Jockey Club to offer a Kentucky version of the English Epsom Derby. Horse racing was almost outlawed in the U.S. in the nineteenth century because of corrupt betting practices. It was saved from that fate through the introduction of a new French parimutuel system, and Churchill Downs was one of the first American race tracks to use it. The famous Twin Spires have graced and characterized the track since 1895.

Caufield and Shook Collection 127658 – 1933

A $121 million renovation and expansion of Churchill Downs completed in 2005 retained the Twin Spires while adding premier seating, suites and other amenities expected in a modern sporting facility. Despite the scale and duration of the remodeling, it proceeded without interrupting Churchill Down's 130-year record of hosting America's longest-running sporting event, the Kentucky Derby, on the first Saturday in May.

GERMANTOWN / HEITZMAN'S BAKERY

1000 Block of East Burnett Avenue

German immigrants settled in an area of Louisville along East Burnett Avenue beginning in the 1850s. Roman Catholic, and sometimes targets of violent discrimination, they lived separately from Protestant German immigrants who had arrived earlier. Roman Catholic parishes like St. Elizabeth's Church on Burnett, shown in this 1952 photograph, provided a focus for community life as well as worship and education. Ironically, Germantown, as the neighborhood came to be known, was built on land considered a swamp but it came to be celebrated for its trim lawns, immaculate shotgun houses, and clean-swept sidewalks and streets. One former resident remembers her mother sweeping the bare ground of a spot in the yard where children's play had worn away the grass. "She was so clean, she even swept the dirt!"

Caufield and Shook Collection 267881 – 1952

Charles Heitzman's Bakery, "Home of Those Famous Wedding and Birthday Cakes," has since moved from this original location but has stores throughout Louisville. Another Germantown landmark, Check's Cafe, still stands across the street, serving its famous bean soup and brats. St. Elizabeth's Church serves parishioners from the Germantown, Schnitzelberg, and Preston neighborhoods.

HIGHLANDS

Bardstown Road, at Baxter and Highland Avenues

Once a turnpike outside Louisville's city limits, Bardstown Road gained electric trolley service in 1889 to further development of the Cherokee Triangle. Developers James Henning and Joshua Speed surveyed and founded the residential area in 1871, but in the 20th century those first elegant homes along Bardstown Road gave way to shops and businesses. Built at the intersection of Bardstown Road and Baxter and Highland Avenues in 1938, the Dahlem Center was considered one of Louisville's earliest shopping centers. In this 1950 photograph, Walgreen's drug store stood at the corner and a Kroger grocery store secured the other end of the center.

Royal Photo Studio Collection 11671 – 1950.

In the 1980s, the Highland's Kroger store moved further out on Bardstown Road, near Doup's Point. In a 2001 renovation of the Dahlem Center, Walgreens moved down the row of shops into more spacious quarters closer to St. Brigid's Catholic Church on Hepburn Avenue. A Starbucks coffee house, a Cold Stone Creamery ice cream shop and other small businesses in the Center continue to serve the retail needs of the neighborhood today.

HIGHLANDS / CARMICHAEL'S BOOKSTORE

1200 Block of Bardstown Road, at Longest Avenue

In this 1930s photograph, trolley tracks run down the middle of Bardstown Road, once a bricked street and former turnpike toll road. On this particular corner, Longest Avenue opened wide so that street cars could pass as they turned off Bardstown Road toward Cherokee Park. Oatey-Forbes Drugs occupied the corner at this time and, in the 1960s, the same site was home to Neubauer Drugs.

R.G. Potter Collection 2357 – circa 1930

Carmichael's, Louisville's oldest continuously-operating independent bookstore, opened on the corner of Bonnycastle Avenue and Bardstown Road in 1978. The shop moved to the corner of Bardstown Road and Longest Avenue in 1983. Ramsi's Café on the World, on the north side of the store, reflects the range of ethnic cuisines now available in Louisville Metro, and is one of the many dining establishments along Bardstown Road giving rise to the street's identification as Louisville's "Restaurant Row." In 1994, Heine Brothers Coffee opened its first store on this corner, behind Carmichael's. Its front door opens onto Longest Avenue and it is a favorite neighborhood gathering place for coffee and conversation.

HIGHLANDS / THE SCHUSTER BUILDING

Bardstown Road at Eastern Parkway

Built in 1927, the Schuster Building on Bardstown Road housed the Uptown, a popular neighborhood movie theater, along with a grocery, delicatessen, drug store and other shops and offices. In this 1949 photograph, the marquee of the Uptown advertises a double bill of *Green Promises* and *Stagecoach Kid*. The Uptown faltered as suburban multiplex theaters with larger screens and more parking boomed in popularity during the 1970s and 1980s.

Caufield and Shook Collection 247520 – 1949

Model Drugs was one of the original shops in the Schuster Building when it opened as a shopping center in 1928. The store offered home delivery, a soda fountain and a circulating library.

R.G. Potter Collection 2375.1 – 1930

LOUISVILLE 168 THEN AND NOW

By the late 1980s, developers planned to demolish the Schuster Building, along with the Uptown, but local businessman Ed Hart teamed up with the city to rehabilitate the structure into retail shops and offices. Although the theater itself was demolished and the Uptown sign removed, the movie marquee remains.

After the Schuster Building's 1989 renovation, the corner of the building housed a bagel shop and now, a Qdoba Mexican Grill. The busy restaurant opens out onto the corner of Eastern Parkway and Bardstown Road, which also provides one of Louisville Metro's many Bright Spots. These small parks, located throughout the city, have been created as one of Mayor Jerry Abramson's Brightside initiatives and are maintained by their neighbors.

HIGHLANDS / CHEROKEE TRIANGLE / CASTLEMAN STATUE

Cherokee Road at Cherokee Parkway

General John Breckinridge Castleman (1841-1918) fought with Confederate General John Hunt Morgan during the Civil War. Following a period of post-war exile in Europe, he returned to Louisville to establish a distinguished career in civic life. As president of the Board of Parks Commission, General Castleman not only led the effort to establish the city's park system, but he commissioned Frederick Law Olmsted to design Louisville's parks, which now comprise one of the most extensive group of Olmsted parks in the country. General Castleman lived to attend the unveiling of his statue in Cherokee Park in 1913.

R.G. Potter Collection 1932 – circa 1928

The Castleman statue today anchors the traffic roundabout on Cherokee Parkway at Cherokee Road, in the heart of the neighborhood known as the Cherokee Triangle. A local children's legend holds that his horse shifts its stance to its other hooves at midnight on Halloween.

HIGHLANDS / CHEROKEE PARK / DANIEL BOONE STATUE

Cherokee Park at Eastern Parkway

Cherokee Park was designed by Frederick Law Olmsted's landscape design firm. Olmsted, on his first visit to Louisville in 1891, proclaimed it a "beautifully endowed landscape." Much like Central Park in New York, Cherokee Park was, and is, a large forested greenspace meant to provide shade, walking and biking paths, and leisure space to those who live on its perimeter. Cherokee Park is home to features like Big Rock, Hogan's Fountain and the Enid Yandell sculpture of Daniel Boone. The park's beautiful old trees were devastated by Louisville's 1974 tornado (above), which entered the park directly over Boone's head.

With help from the Louisville Metro Parks Department, spirited civic groups like Trees, Inc. and the Olmsted Conservancy, Cherokee Park has gradually re-forested and re-grown in the years since the 1974 tornado. Cherokee Park provides visitors with a wide array of amenities including a golf course, an archery range, a rugby field, basketball courts, and a 2.4 mile Scenic Loop, with separate lanes for vehicle and recreational traffic. Vehicles driving the Loop can leave the park by continually turning right, or remain in the park by continually turning left.

HIGHLANDS / BARDSTOWN ROAD AT MIDLAND AVENUE

Indian Gas Refineries maintained filling stations around Louisville through the 1930s, including this one at Bardstown Road and Midland Avenue. They came to be identified as sellers of Texaco products.

R.G. Potter Collection 3221.2 – circa 1933

A chain convenience store occupies the corner of Bardstown Road and Midland Avenue today, but the Besten Apartment House, built circa 1905 and largely unchanged, still stands to the east of the corner business. Off in the distance, on the right in this photograph, is 1400 Willow—a 21-story condominium complex overlooking Cherokee Park that is home to many retired civic leaders and others who enjoy the convenience of condominium living in the city's vibrant Cherokee Triangle neighborhood.

BARDSTOWN ROAD / DOUGLASS LOOP

Bardstown Road at Dundee and Douglass Boulevard

The Douglass Loop was named for Western Union executive George Lattimore Douglass, whose estate spread over the area, and for the turning loop which allowed the street car line to bring passengers to the new suburban area beginning in 1912. By the 1920s, new subdivisions—including Lakeside and Strathmoor—were growing off Bardstown Road, providing a customer base for a rich mix of shops springing up around the Douglass Loop.

Caufield and Shook Collection 148019 – 1936

Over the years, the offerings in the triangle of land within the Douglass Loop and on the adjacent streets have been broad—groceries, meats, fruits and delicatessen fare; flowers, antiques and ladies' ready to wear. New businesses such as Cakes by Helen and Heine Brothers Coffee have joined traditional stores in the "Loop." Local residents rely on Horton's Hardware and Douglass Pharmacy, which occupy the corner at Dundee.

TYLER PARK

Tyler Park, named after Louisville Mayor Henry S. Tyler (1851-1896) opened in 1910. The park, developed around a distinctive bridge, was designed by landscape architect John Olmsted and constructed by Louisville city employees in 1904. The neighborhood flourished as a late 19th-century street car suburb and was well established when this 1921 photograph of the park's popular tennis courts was taken.

Caufield and Shook Collection 38356 – 1921

Tyler Park's dimensions have remained unchanged over time, but its look has changed as its trees have matured. The Tyler Park tennis courts, which produced 14 state tennis champions, remain popular today. In 2004, the Tyler Park Neighborhood Association celebrated the area's 100-year history in the park.

REPUBLIC BANK & TRUST COMPANY
2800 Block of Bardstown Road

Cited as a model for cooperation with an historic neighborhood, Republic Bank's original building on Bardstown Road involved saving and renovating a neglected structure on a prominent corner of Strathmoor Village. For much of its history, this building in the 2800 block of Bardstown Road served as a neighborhood restaurant, beginning with Salvatore Denunzio's Diner (below) from 1928 to 1933.

R.G. Potter Collection 1877 – 1928

Republic Bank and Trust Company, chartered in 1982, today operates as one of the few banks with headquarters in Louisville. Republic Bank now has more than 30 branches throughout Kentucky and southern Indiana.

Top photos on both pages courtesy of Republic Bank

DOUP'S POINT

Taylorsville Road at Bardstown Road

Doup's Point—at the intersection of Bardstown Road, Taylorsville Road and Trevilian Way—bears the name of Daniel Doup, who owned the farmland near this intersection when the area boasted the world's largest onion farm. In this 1935 image and still today, a Standard Oil/Chevron service station is located in Doup's Point, on the slight rise in the curve toward Louisville on Bardstown Road. The Brenzel family has operated the neighborhood service station since 1973.

Louisville Herald Post Collection 94.18.1075 – 1935.

Diagonally across Bardstown Road, Walgreen's Pharmacy has replaced a bank on the southwest corner at Trevilian Way. Steiden's grocery store occupied the corner until the 1950s. A McDonald's restaurant is now located on the northwest corner, across Taylorsville Road from Brenzel's service station. The Doup family cemetery remains today, just two short blocks further out Bardstown Road.

BELLARMINE UNIVERSITY

2000 Block of Newburg Road

The largest private institution of higher learning in the Commonwealth, Bellarmine College was founded in 1950 by Archbishop John A. Floersh and sponsored by the Catholic Archdiocese of Louisville as a liberal arts college for men. The college was named for Cardinal Robert Bellarmine, a 17th-century Italian Jesuit priest who was canonized in 1922. Its first president, the Reverend (later Monsignor) Alfred F. Horrigan, served from 1950 to 1973. The Bellarmine College Administration Building, pictured above, was renamed Horrigan Hall in his honor.

Photos courtesy of Bellarmine University

The school was open to all races and, after its merger with east Louisville's Ursuline College in 1968, became coeducational. Known briefly as Ursuline-Bellarmine College, the school returned to the name Bellarmine College in 1971, and began to develop graduate programs in 1975. In recognition of its status as a Masters I institution, the College's Board of Trustees voted to change the institution's name to Bellarmine University in 2000. Bellarmine leaders recently announced a new goal to become the premier independent Catholic university in the South by 2020.

BOWMAN FIELD

2800 Block of Taylorsville Road

In 1919, A.H. Bowman leased 50 acres of land to establish an airfield on what was formerly the estate of Konrad von Zedwitz, a German count whose holdings were confiscated by the federal government during World War I. Three years later, the U.S. Army took over Bowman's lease, and by 1923 the rudimentary airdrome was known as Bowman Field. In 1927, the Louisville Board of Trade supported government ownership of Bowman Field and passed a bond issue to purchase the entire von Zedwitz property. Most of the land became Seneca Park, but the rest was given over to Bowman Field, which quickly became a hub of commercial aviation. By 1929, paved runways and a brick passenger terminal were completed.

Caufield and Shook Collection 106268 – 1929

Today Bowman Field, the oldest airport in Kentucky, is still in operation for corporate and private flights. It is also home to Kosair Children's Hospital's StatCare Transport Team, providing emergency transportation services to the hospital for babies and children in the surrounding region. The former passenger terminal has been renovated into offices, but mainly it is the home of Le Relais, a fine French restaurant. Just across the street is the Air Devil's Inn, a bar and restaurant made popular during the World War II years when Bowman Field was a training airfield.

BIG ROCK / CHEROKEE PARK

Big Rock, located on the middle fork of Beargrass Creek in Louisville's Cherokee Park, has been a favorite destination for family picnics and youth activities for generations. Children have fished for "crawdads," and teens have used the swings and stones as props for romantic encounters since the 1890s, when the city added the eastern boundary of what had been George Douglass' property to Cherokee Park. The mill stones from old Ward's Mill survive on the opposite shore of the creek, just above Big Rock.

H.C. Griswold Collection 1979.26.098 – circa 1895

Beargrass Creek floods often, changing the rocks and pools in the creek, but Big Rock remains a favorite destination for waders, hikers and climbers. Big Rock continues to be one of Cherokee Park's favorite picnic and playground locations. Each October, the Highland-Douglass Big Rock Jazz Festival is hosted in the band shelter adjacent to Big Rock.

ST. MATTHEWS / LEXINGTON ROAD / VOGUE THEATER

3700 Block of Lexington Road

R.G. Potter Collection 6029 – 1939

Royal Photo Studio Collection 5005.03 – 1939

The area in the East End of Louisville known as St. Matthews took its name from the Episcopal church in the area. One of its main corridors, Lexington Road, was constructed in the mid-1800s as a shortcut to downtown. The area where Lexington Road and Frankfort Avenue converge in St. Matthews was known as The Point. A gas station at the apex of The Point has been there for several generations. Further west, the owners of Taylor Drugs built the complex of stores along Lexington Road in 1939 as "a modern community project." The center served for decades as part of St. Matthews' retail hub with an F. W. Woolworth's and the Vogue Theater as major tenants. Across Lexington Road stood such popular stores as Byck's, Buster Brown Shoes and a restaurant called The Canary Cottage.

In 2005, the owners of the center announced plans to renovate the complex and to save the landmark Vogue Theater sign. The center now houses a Homemade Ice Cream and Pie Kitchen and other specialty shops and stands at the center of St. Matthews' new "Corridor of Opportunity." A variety of bank branches and new retail stores are now located across the street.

Photos courtesy of Scott Stortz

ST. MATTHEWS / PLEHN'S BAKERY

3900 Block of Shelbyville Road

Kuno Plehn, a baker who had emigrated from Germany to the United States, opened his bakery at Shelbyville Road and Meridian Avenue in 1924. This view looking east on Shelbyville Road was taken in 1933. The businesses on the north side of the former turnpike that linked Louisville with Shelbyville have changed dramatically over the years, but Plehn's Bakery has remained a reliable St. Matthew's landmark for generations.

Caufield and Shook Collection 126351 – 1933

Today, the bakery maintains one of Louisville's very few remaining soda fountain counters and still offers its signature kuchen which has long been a Sunday morning staple in local homes. Over the years, Plehn's has graced thousands of marriages with their artful wedding cakes. Their famous iced sugar cookies, decorated to celebrate seasons and holidays, continue to delight children and adults.

ST. MATTHEWS / SHELBYVILLE ROAD

3900 Block of Shelbyville Road

For many years, St. Matthews was a center of potato-growing and the site of a large produce exchange. This west-facing view of Shelbyville Road in the heart of St. Matthews in the 1930s shows a bustling row of shops on the south side, much like it is today. The area just north of this location, between Shelbyville Road and Brownsboro Road, was just beginning to be transformed from farmland into housing tracts. Very quickly, St. Matthews became the largest of Louisville's suburban neighborhoods. City annexation attempts prompted St. Matthews to incorporate as a sixth-class city in 1950, with a leap to fourth-class city status five years later.

Caufield and Shook Collection 138860 – 1935

Today, the Shelbyville Road corridor in St. Matthews is one of the busiest traffic areas in Louisville Metro. The blocks between St. Matthews Avenue and Hubbards Lane are comprised of shops, banks, restaurants, car dealerships and Trinity High School, established in 1953 and growing ever larger on its campus on Shelbyville Road at Sherrin Avenue.

ST. MATTHEWS / PRYOR'S RESTAURANT / ARBY'S

4100 Block of Shelbyville Road, at Hubbards Lane

In this 1952 photograph, Pryor's Restaurant—at the intersection of Shelbyville Road and Hubbards Lane—was a popular east-end eatery, offering steaks, shakes, fried chicken and biscuits with honey. In a time when most families still ate meals at home, Pryor's provided an alternative, with optional in-car service, and helped transform Louisville into a community with residents who eat out often. Webb's Drug Store was located across the street from Pryor's, on the southeast corner of Shelbyville Road and Hubbard's Lane.

Royal Photo Studio Collection 13404.01 – 1952

Today the corner of Shelbyville Road and Hubbard's Lane in St. Matthews is still a food corner, but it is now an Arby's restaurant. The former Webb's Drug Store has changed hands several times but remains a pharmacy in the center of one of Louisville's largest post-World War II neighborhoods.

MALL ST. MATTHEWS

Shelbyville Road at the Watterson Expressway

Louisville's first indoor shopping center, The Mall, opened in 1962 across from the East Drive-In on Shelbyville Road. The Mall was the first of the commercial centers to cater to post-World War II suburbanites who liked to shop at stores convenient to their homes. They felt free to dress more casually when shopping at The Mall than they did when they went downtown, and they enjoyed free parking which was not available in the city. Planning began almost immediately for Oxmoor Mall, which opened in 1971 further east on Shelbyville Road, on a 34-acre portion of the Bullitt family estate.

Caufield and Shook Collection C-0934.3 – 1962

With the opening of these shopping malls, St. Matthews started stretching east toward Middletown and Anchorage, establishing a line of housing and commercial space that today runs unbroken along Shelbyville Road. The Mall has undergone many renovations in its 40+ years, and some tenants change from year to year. The complex has become a regional retail center as St. Matthews has grown and subdivisions have sprung up all around it.

BAUERS RESTAURANT / AZALEA RESTAURANT

3600 Block of Brownsboro Road

Once one of Louisville's favorite restaurants, Bauers Since 1870 began as a sideline of another business. In the 19th century, the Bauer family was manufacturing wagons on Brownsboro Road, near an area called Indian Hills, when they began to make and sell sandwiches as a convenience for employees crafting the wagons. As the automobile replaced travel by wagon, the Bauers adapted by opening a service station on the site of the old wagon factory and then by offering meals to people traveling out Brownsboro Road by car. Residential development grew, including the communities of Indian Hills and Rolling Fields, and so did the restaurant and its reputation.

Royal Photo Studio Collection 8338 – 1944

After the Bauer family sold the restaurant and the surrounding land (upon which stood a Gateway grocery store, later to become Doll's Market), the building was reborn as a restaurant called La Paloma, and still later as another restaurant called Azalea, which continues the tradition of fine dining on this site. The service station has been razed to provide additional parking for the popular eatery.

CRESCENT HILL RESERVOIR

Reservoir Avenue, Between Frankfort Avenue and Brownsboro Road

In 1879, the Louisville Water Company began to pump river water from the pumping station at River Road up Pipe Line Avenue, across Brownsboro Road to be stored in the new settling basins. Pipe Line Avenue was later renamed Zorn Avenue for Sebastian Zorn, a leader in the grain business who, as president of the Louisville Water Company, was greatly responsible for its modern filtration system and the Crescent Hill swimming pool. Before the reservoir was constructed, customers allowed their tap water to sit so that sediments could sink to the bottom. The elaborate pumping station at the reservoir is adorned with water pitchers and other architectural details that make walking or jogging around the track a visually pleasing experience. The recent re-lining of the two basins revealed that the architects' attention to detail went beyond the design of the pumping station on the site. When the basins were emptied, workers found that even the submerged intake pipes were decorated with elaborate Gothic Revival detailing.

Caufield and Shook Collection 6974 – circa 1915

Security concerns in 2002 demanded that a new fence be constructed around the Crescent Hill Reservoir, but the cement pathways around the two settling ponds still provide flat walking/jogging lanes for recreational users. The Gothic Revival building remains unchanged from its 1879 construction. Louisville's tornado of 1974 caused considerable damage to the buildings and grounds, but subsequent repairs preserved all the original details.

CRESCENT HILL / FRANKFORT AVENUE

Frankfort Avenue at Bayly

By 1923, Crescent Hill had been incorporated into the City of Louisville, but inhabitants of the area nevertheless thought of themselves as belonging to a tightly-knit community. Hinkebein's Pharmacy was a favorite hangout for Crescent Hill youth, and local residents relied upon Mr. Hinkebein's expertise to dispense drugs to cure most common ailments. In this photo, the tracks of the interurban rail line run past the site of the Piggly Wiggly grocery operating in the white building just to the east.

Caufield and Shook Collection 48786 – 1923

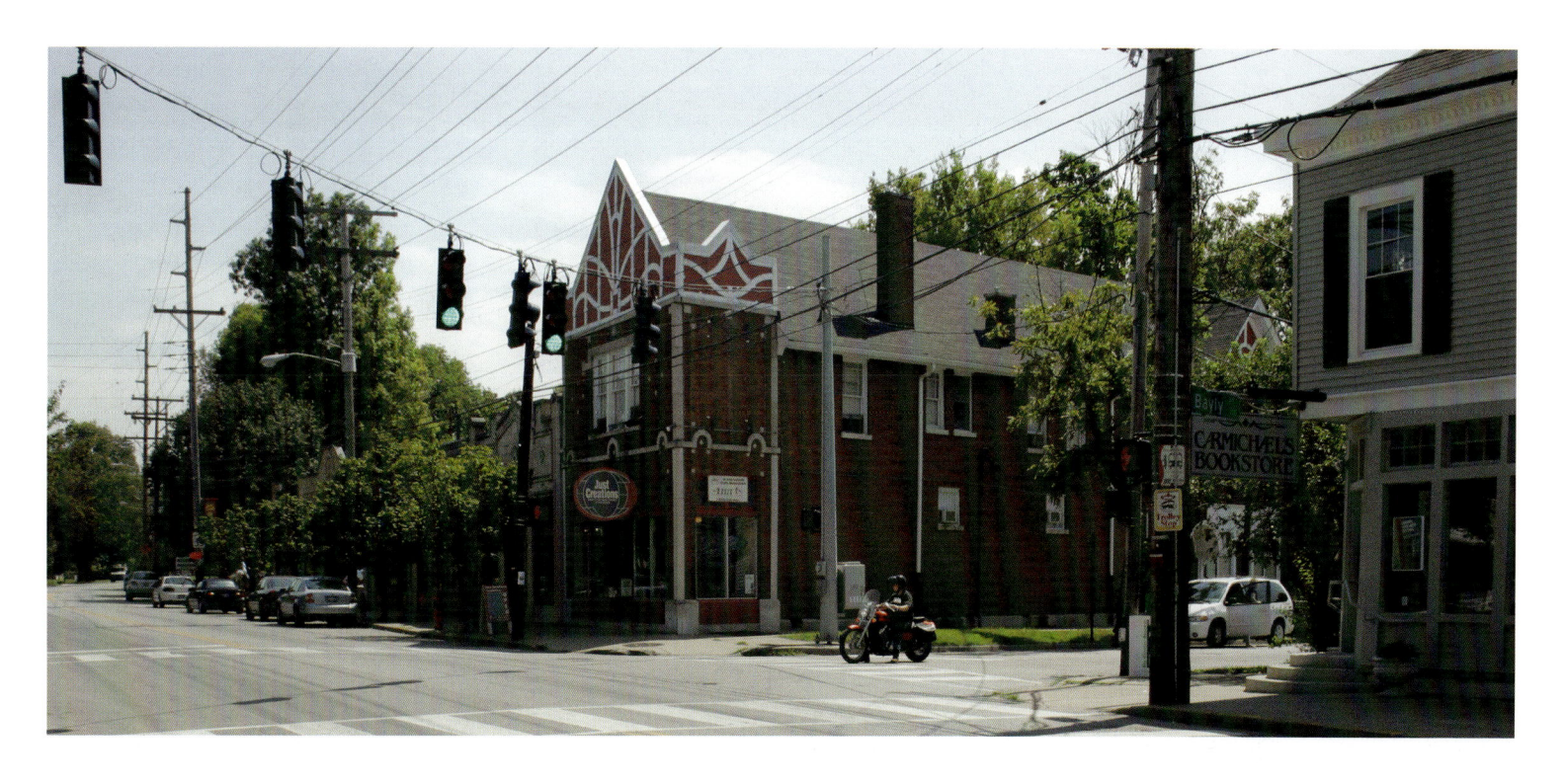

Today Hinkebein's Pharmacy is the site of Just Creations, a store featuring unique hand-crafted items from around the globe. Across Bayly, where Hudson's Grocery was located, is another Carmichael's locally-owned bookstore.

CRESCENT HILL / FRANKFORT AVENUE

2700 Block of Frankfort Avenue

Business storefronts altered the faces of structures along Frankfort Avenue on the south side of the old turnpike between Bayly and Hite Avenues. For years, residents could buy any goods or services they wanted or needed at these neighborhood stores.

R.G. Potter Collection 6070 – circa 1940

Frankfort Avenue today is bustling with shops and popular restaurants. A new building housing the Wine Rack has replaced Allison's Ice Cream stand. A new gelato and ice cream emporium, however, has opened just east of the Wine Rack.

CRESCENT HILL / STEAM ENGINE COMPANY NO. 21

Frankfort Avenue at Franck

Steam Engine Company No. 21 at the corner of Frankfort and Franck Avenues, was built in 1907-08. A local resident sacrificed a popular neighborhood tennis court to clear space for the firehouse and equipment. Historian Samuel W. Thomas found one Crescent Hill resident who remembered the time when not only firefighters, but also three horses, were housed at the firehouse.

R.G. Potter Collection 1769 – 1930

The corner of Frankfort and Franck Avenues still houses a neighborhood fire station, now just shy of celebrating its 100th birthday.

BUTCHERTOWN

Frankfort Avenue at Story Avenue

The intersection of the bricked road joining Frankfort and Story Avenues forms a gateway to Butchertown, one of Louisville's largest German settlements. In the late 1900s the area around this view of Seitz Drugs began to become popular, as creative local residents rehabilitated houses and business venues. In this photograph, the man at left is looking at the demolition of the Bray-Robinson Clothing Company which operated, alongside the Semple Manufacturing Company (makers of girths, blankets and twine), into the 20th century.

Caufield and Shook Collection 21200 – 1945

Several decades back, two buildings on Story Avenue, including the one that housed Seitz Drugs, were removed to create direct access to the river down Ohio Street. Old Ohio Street, which connected to River Road, was re-named Frankfort Avenue to give the Frankfort Avenue corridor a continuous identity from River Road to St. Matthews.

BUTCHERTOWN / FORMER OERTEL'S BREWERY

1300 Block of Story Avenue

The German immigrants who began to flock to the area now known as Butchertown in the early 1800s brought skills in the brewing arts. By the turn of the century, several breweries flourished in the neighborhood, including Franklin Brewery on Franklin Street, Oertel's and Steurer's Breweries on Story Avenue, and Clifton Brewery on Brownsboro Road at Ewing Avenue. Oertel's Brewery became the best known of these establishments. Their popular Oertel's '92 brand of pale lager, introduced around 1935, was synonymous with the brewery itself. The brewery was sold to the Brown-Forman Corporation in 1964. Finding that the modernization of the old bottling works would not be a prudent investment, Brown-Forman decided to close Oertel's in 1967.

Royal Photo Studio Collection 7206.01 – 1942

A subsequent effort by former Oertel's brewmaster Friedrich W. "Fritz" Finger, Jr. and other partners to open a microbrewery proved ahead of its time. Today, however, the building has found new use as the offices of an event management firm.

STOTTMAN'S CAFE & GRILL / BAXTER STATION BAR AND GRILL

1201 Payne Street

Louisville has long been a city of neighborhoods. These communities within the community provide inhabitants with a sense of belonging, a feeling that can prove elusive in a large metropolitan area like Louisville. Neighborhood schools, churches and restaurants provide opportunities for residents to gather and build connections. Corner taverns were a part of life in most Louisville neighborhoods. Formerly known as Joyce's Pub, and in the 1950s as Stottmann's Café & Grill, this neighborhood hangout is located on a street named after Ward Payne, who subdivided the surrounding property in 1864.

Royal Photo Studio Collection 11725 – 1950

The popular neighborhood bar and restaurant is now called the Baxter Station Bar and Grill. Its name comes from the old Baxter Station railroad depot, the remains of which are nearby at Lexington Road and Chestnut Street.

MIDDLETOWN / LITTLE BIT OF BYBEE POTTERY

11617 Main Street (Old Shelbyville Road)

Middletown got its name from being either midway between Louisville and Shelbyville or between Westport and Shippingport. Regardless, the community was established in 1797 as a stagecoach stop. Structures like the Davis Tavern, also known as the Wetherby House, and the Benjamin Head House have lined its Main Street since the early 19th century. Later in that century an interurban line connected the town to Louisville. Although a 1930s move to build U.S. Highway 60 to the north instead of along Main Street was criticized at the time, many credit that decision for being the reason so many of Middletown's historic buildings were saved, including this grocery, Mason Grocery & Supply Company, in an unidentified night-time Prohibition-era photograph.

Caufield and Shook Collection 129921 – 1933

The building, like other survivors on Main Street, has remained in constant use and enjoys new life today as a home for Bybee Pottery. The distinctive crockery is nearly as old as Middletown, dating back to 1809 when a pottery was first established in Madison County, Kentucky. The Cornelius family still operates kilns in Bybee, Kentucky, but has established this outpost, Little Bit of Bybee Pottery, in Middletown. Sidewalks and other streetscape improvements are currently being built along Middletown's US Highway 60 bypass.

ANCHORAGE / ANCHORAGE SCHOOL

11000 Block of Ridge Road

Caufield and Shook Collection 183139 – 1941

The community of Anchorage, Kentucky got its name from a steamboat anchor mounted in the front yard of early resident and ship captain James Goslee. In 1912, Citizens National Life Insurance Company built Jefferson County's first suburban office building in Anchorage. Kentucky Central Life and Accident Insurance Company purchased the building in 1917.

Southern Pacific Railroad took advantage of Kentucky's favorable tax rates by maintaining its headquarters in the state, although it had no actual railroad tracks or trains here. The railroad leased one room and held annual meetings in the Kentucky Central Building from 1915 until 1931. After Kentucky Central moved to Lexington in 1973, the graceful stucco building housed the Louisville School of Art until the school became part of the University of Louisville Hite Art Institute. Today the building offers gracious office space under the name of Anchorage Crossings.

Louisville Herald Post Collection 1994.18.0263 – 1936

The interurban rail line facilitated late-19th-century development of Anchorage around the estate of Edward D. Hobbs. To educate their children, residents opened Anchorage Common Graded School in 1911. The school moved to its current location in 1915. Supported by tax revenue from the Southern Pacific Railroad, Anchorage School provided education for all grades until 1950, when high school students moved to the then-new Eastern High School in Middletown that opened to accommodate the post World War II "baby-boomer" generation. Anchorage School consistently achieves top rankings among Kentucky's public schools.

JEFFERSONTOWN

Taylorsville Road at Watterson Trail

In 1797, Jefferson County approved Abraham Bruner's petition to found Brunerstown within his 122 acres in the far eastern section of the county. The community soon became known as Jeffersontown, and was one of only three incorporated municipalities in the county, the others being Louisville (1780) and Anchorage (1878). Jeffersontown's growth and development resulted from the construction of the electric interurban train lines that emanated from Louisville's city center in the early 1900s. These train lines made commuting easy, and thousands of Louisvillians took advantage and moved to the idyllic countryside to become residents of such towns as Middletown, Anchorage, Okolona and Jeffersontown.

Louisville Herald Post Collection 1994.18.0335 – 1920

In the 1950s, the old Louisville-Taylorsville Turnpike which led to Jeffersontown's public square was widened and automobile traffic increased. Jeffersontown today, like other outlying communities, is decidedly less rural than it was in its beginnings. As Louisville has expanded to the east, Jeffersontown has built shopping malls, movie theaters and restaurants. The city has also developed large industrial parks over the years that generate significant tax revenues. Jeffersontown's annual Gaslight Festival draws thousands of visitors to the community each September.

HARRODS CREEK

River Road at Wolf Pen Branch Road

Established as a stop for Ohio River cargo to be unloaded to proceed overland into Kentucky or around the Falls of the Ohio, Harrods Creek started to develop as a community when the Louisville, Harrods Creek and Westport Railroad began operation in 1877. The community enjoyed another boost when the advent of the interurban line in 1904 made it easier to move between homes in Harrods Creek and businesses in downtown Louisville. In addition to homes and estates, Harrods Creek has also been something of a dining center, with Captain's Quarters, the Chick Inn, the former Bus Parson's River Creek Inn and the Pine Room situated close together on River Road. This 1935 image shows Robertson's Grocery, at the fork of River Road and Wolf Pen Branch Road, which also served as the community's post office and informal communication center.

Louisville Herald Post Collection 1994.18.1093 – 1935

Today the grocery is long gone and the building has served many different owners over the last 70 years. The road is still well-traveled, with eastbound cars turning left to cross the Harrods Creek bridge or going straight up Wolf Pen Branch toward St. Francis in the Fields Episcopal Church, U.S. Highway 42 and the Gene Snyder Freeway. This area will soon be home to a new Ohio River bridge that will connect the Gene Snyder Freeway to Indiana.

IROQUOIS MANOR SHOPPING CENTER

5300 Block of South Third Street

During World War II, war industries like Naval Ordnance stimulated growth in Louisville. Built as a suburban shopping center for post-World War II residents constructing new homes in south Louisville, Iroquois Manor was thriving in 1964 when this photograph documented a new Winn-Dixie supermarket.

Royal Photo Studio Collection 18502.03 – 1964

After a period of decline, Iroquois Manor is again a vibrant neighborhood center, also known throughout Louisville as the location of the Vietnam Kitchen restaurant and Valu Market, a grocery featuring an extensive selection of ethnic foods. The neighborhood has changed too, becoming one of Louisville's most diverse communities. The nearby Americana Apartment Complex has developed into the city's largest refugee resettlement site. Vietnamese, Bosnian, Cuban and Sudanese immigrants are among the many new citizens of Louisville creating a richly diverse neighborhood where 19 different languages are spoken. At the heart of the neighborhood is the Americana Community Center, which assists international residents with classes and services that help them establish new lives in Louisville. The Center hosts an annual international festival in September which showcases ethnic foods, crafts and entertainment and draws thousands of people from throughout the community.

KFC / YUM! BRANDS, INC. HEADQUARTERS

1900 Colonel Sanders Lane

Colonel Harland Sanders developed his famous fried chicken recipe in Corbin, Kentucky, where he operated a service station and restaurant. By 1955, he had established a franchise with his Original Recipe Kentucky Fried Chicken. In 1964, Colonel Sanders sold the recipe and his business to John Y. Brown, Jr., an entrepreneur who took the fried chicken, and the Colonel's distinctive image, worldwide. Brown opened the white-pillared Kentucky Fried Chicken headquarters off Gardiner Lane in Louisville in 1970. The adjoining Colonel Sanders Technical Center, with vials of the Colonel's famous secret blend of herbs and spices embedded in the cornerstone, opened in 1986.

Royal Photo Studio Collection 19558 – 1970

Photo provided by Yum! Brands, Inc.

John Y. Brown, Jr. sold the KFC Corporation to Heublein, Inc. in 1971, which was acquired by R.J Reynolds Industries, Inc. (now RJR Nabisco, Inc.) in 1982. PepsiCo acquired KFC in 1986, then spun KFC, Taco Bell and Pizza Hut into Tricon Global Restaurants, Inc. in 1997. The company's name was changed to Yum! Brands, Inc. in 2002. Today, the Yum! Brands family is comprised of over 34,000 restaurants in 100 countries that generated over $9 billion in total sales and franchise revenues in 2005. The company is still headquartered in Louisville, Kentucky, in the original KFC headquarters. Testing continues to be conducted in KFC's special test restaurants, where the public is often invited to sample and give opinions on new foods and old favorites.

Photos on this page provided by Yum! Brands, Inc.

FORD MOTOR COMPANY

Caufield and Shook Collection 165533 – 1939

Photo courtesy of Ford Motor Company

© *The Courier-Journal, Michael Hayman*

Ford Motor Company produced Model T's at Louisville's first auto assembly plant, built in 1916 at Third and Eastern Parkway (top photo). Although production was suspended during World War I while the plant was used for war efforts, it resumed in 1919 and, by 1925, moved to a new plant on Southwestern Parkway (middle photo). After making another contribution to the national effort building Army vehicles during World War II (top photo, opposite page), Ford built new plants: an automobile assembly plant in 1955 at Fern Valley Road and Grade Lane (above); and a truck assembly plant in 1969, off Westport Road on Chamberlain Lane.

Lin Caufield Collection LC 45-0067-01 – 1945

Photo courtesy of Ford Motor Company

Louisville Ford plants have produced 11 million vehicles: Model T's and Model A's, heavy trucks and LTD's, Rangers and Explorers. Ford celebrated its two millionth truck rolling off its assembly line in Kentucky in 1995 (above photo). A recent $65 million re-tooling of the assembly line now allows the Louisville Truck Plant to build most models of Ford sport utility vehicles and all models of Ford trucks.

GENERAL ELECTRIC APPLIANCE PARK

This 1955 kitchen shows one of GE's "Mix-Or-Match Colors" introduced for GE's full line of major appliances. These colors included Petal Pink, Canary Yellow, Cadet Blue, Turquoise Green and Woodtone Brown.

Photo courtesy of GE

When, in 1950, General Electric decided to create one location for manufacturing its appliances, the company found that Louisville offered location, labor, and transportation systems necessary for success. Appliance Park, spreading over nearly 1000 acres, opened in Buechel in 1952.

Struck Construction Company Collection neg. 1651 – 1950

This kitchen represents current offerings from GE Profile™, an appliance line that marries the best in both style and innovation. Products include the GE Profile Side by Side Refrigerator with ClimateKeeper2™ technology, the GE Profile Dishwasher with SmartDispense™ technology, the GE Profile Wall Oven with Trivection™ Technology, the GE Profile Advantium® wall oven, and the GE Profile Wine Center.

Photo courtesy of GE

GE recently celebrated the 50th anniversary of Appliance Park. Today Appliance Park, as General Electric's global headquarters for appliances, manufactures the company's cutting-edge products, including the popular Profile lines. The company also develops more than 100 new products a year, making GE the appliance designer to the world. In 2004, GE announced it would locate it's Consumer and Industrial Appliances headquarters at Appliance Park in Louisville.

COCA-COLA BOTTLING COMPANY OF LOUISVILLE

1600 Block of West Hill Street

The Schmidt family established Coca-Cola Bottling Company of Louisville at Tenth and Main Streets in 1901. From this plant, only the second Coca-Cola operation in the nation, Coca-Cola grew to open ever-larger operations in 1912 at 16th and Bank, and in 1941 at 1661 West Hill Street.

Caufield and Shook Collection 28742 - 1955

Coca-Cola Bottling Company, in its 65th year at 1661 West Hill Street, has made Louisville a source for the quintessentially southern soft drink for over a century. Coca-Cola now markets over 350 products and its employees are active and generous contributors to the community.

Pepsi-Cola General Bottlers

Algonquin Parkway/4000 Block of Crittenden Drive

Pepsi-Cola began Louisville operations in 1937 and opened this state-of-the-art bottling plant at 1500 Algonquin Parkway in 1942.

Caufield and Shook Collection neg. 194509 – 1943

Today the Algonquin Parkway building is home to Preiser Scientific, supplier of scientific instruments, laboratory equipment and supplies.

Pepsi-Cola General Bottlers, Inc. of Chicago aquired Pepsi-Cola Louisville Bottlers, Inc in 1956. In 1957, the company built a new plant, still in operation, at 4008 Crittenden Drive. Pepsi and its employees are active and generous supporters of community activities and events.

PAPA JOHN'S INTERNATIONAL, INC.

Now an international enterprise, Papa John's Pizza began in 1984 when young entrepreneur John Schnatter took over a broom closet at the back of his father's tavern in Jeffersonville, Indiana, sold his car to buy equipment, and began making pizzas. Within a year, the fledgling business moved to its own building next door.

Today, with over 2,700 company-owned and franchised restaurants operating in 49 states and 20 international markets, Papa John's ranks as the third-largest pizza company in America.

All photos courtesy of Papa John's International, Inc

The corporate headquarters of Papa John's International, Inc. is now located on 36 acres in Blankenbaker Crossings in Jeffersontown.

L&N SHOPS/CABOOSES AT PAPA JOHN'S CARDINAL STADIUM

2700 Block of South Floyd Street

The Louisville & Nashville Railroad, Louisville's leading railroad, expanded rapidly in the late 1800s. Their first repair shop was acquired by purchasing the Kentucky Locomotive Works at Tenth and Kentucky Streets in 1858. This served the railroad for four decades; however the need for larger facilities necessitated the acquisition of 68 acres in South Louisville, where L&N constructed 20 buildings. During its nearly 90 years of operation, thousands of cars and engines were repaired. In addition, 400 new engines and over 14,000 freight and passenger cars were produced. CSX Transportation, successor to L&N, finally closed the repair facility in 1990.

L&N Railroad Collection 96.20.0654

The University of Louisville's new football stadium, Papa John's Cardinal Stadium, opened on the L&N site in 1998. Used for concerts and community events as well as for University of Louisville Cardinal football games, Papa John's Cardinal Stadium established a new southern boundary for the campus and spurred growth and development in the surrounding neighborhood. Railroad cars parked behind the stadium have been privately purchased and today are used by their owners as pre-game entertainment venues.

Index

Abell Administration Building, UofL HSC 130-131
Acknowledgments 6-7
Actors Theatre of Louisville 52-53
Aegon Tower 34-35
American Life Building 58-59
Anchorage 218-219
Anchorage School 219
Arby's 197
Arena site 76-77
Azalea Restaurant 200-201
BB&T 56-57
Bank of Louisville 52-53
Bank One 26-27
Bardstown Road 164-169, 174-177, 180-183
Bauer's Restaurant 200-201
Baxter Station Bar and Grill 215
Belgravia Court 126-127
Bellarmine University 184-185
Belle of Louisville 80-81
BellSouth 100-101
Belvedere 58-59, 60-61
Big Rock, Cherokee Park 188-189
Boone, Daniel, Statue of 172-173
Bourbon Stock Yards 42-43
Bowman Field 186-187
Brinly-Hardy 44-45
Broaddus, Mayor Andrew, Wharf Boat 80-81
Broadway 102-113, 144-145
Brown Brothers Cadillac 108-109
Brown-Forman Corporation 138-139
Brown Hotel 106-107, 108-109
Butchertown 210-213
Carmichael's Bookstore 167, 205
Carter Dry Goods 68-69
Castleman, General John Breckinridge, Statue of 170-171
Cathedral of the Assumption 122-123
Central Park 124-125
Cherokee Park 172-173, 188-189
Cherokee Triangle 170-171
Churchill Downs 160-161
Citizens Fidelity Bank 24-25
City Hall 14-15
City of Parks initiative 85
Clark, George Rogers, Memorial Bridge 50-51, 74-75
Clarksdale 136
Coast Guard Station #10 80-81
Coca-Cola Bottling Company of Louisville 232-233
Columbia Auditorium 118-119
Courier-Journal 110-111
Crescent Hill 202-209
Crescent Hill Reservoir 202-203
Delta Air Lines 156-157
Denuzio's Diner 180
Dixie Baking Company 145
Dixie Highway 138-139
Douglass Loop 176-177
Doup's Point 182-183
E.ON U.S., LG&E 54-55
E-Main 48-49
Federal Reserve Bank 36-37
Fire Station Number 2 20-21
First National Bank 64-65
First Trust Centre 38-39
Ford Motor Company 228-229
Fourth Street 88-99, 118-119, 124-125
Fourth Street Live! 88-89, 90-91
Frankfort Avenue 204-211
Frazier International History Museum 72-73
Galt House Hotel 78-79
General Electric Appliance Park 230-231
German Bank Building 36-37
Germantown 162-163
Glassworks 40-41
Goldberg's 34-35

Great Lawn, Waterfront Park 86-87
Greater Bethel Temple Apostolic Church 120-121
Greater Louisville Inc. 8-9
Greater Louisville Savings & Building Association 32-33
Harrods Creek 222-223
Heine Brothers' Coffee 167, 207
Heitzman's Bakery 162-163
Heyburn Building 108-109
Highlands 164-177
Hinkebein's Pharmacy 204-205
HSA Broadband Building – Public Radio Partnership 92-93
Hubbuch Brothers & Wellendorff, 92
Humana Building 66-67
Idlewild 80
Index 240
Indian Gas filling station 174
Iroquois Manor Shopping Center 224-225
Iroquois Park 12-13
JPMorgan Chase Bank 26-27
Jefferson Community and Technical College 102-103
Jefferson County Courthouse 16-17
Jefferson Hotel 28-29
Jefferson Street 14-21, 24-29
Jefferson, Thomas, Statue of 18-19
Jeffersontown 220-221
Jewish Hospital & St. Mary's Healthcare 128-129
Just Creations 205
Kaufman-Straus Building 90-91
Kentucky Center 62-63
Kentucky Central Life & Accident Insurance Company 218
Kentucky Electric Company Building 92-93
Kentucky Fair and Exposition Center 152-153
Kentucky Fried Chicken 226-227
Kentucky International Convention Center 28-29
Kentucky Theater 98-99
KFC Headquarters 226-227
Kindred Healthcare 108-109
L&N Shops 238
Lexington Road 190-191
Levy Brothers Building 30-31
Liberty Green 137
Liberty National Bank 26-27
Little Bit of Bybee Pottery 217
Loew's /United Artists State Theatre 96-97
Louisville & Nashville Railroad (L&N) 112, 238
Louisville Fire Department Station Number 2 20-21
Louisville Fire Department Steam Engine Co. No. 21 208-209
Louisville Free Public Library 116-117
Louisville Gas and Electric Company 54-55, 76-77
Louisville International Airport 156-159
Louisville Metro Hall 16-17, 18-19
Louisville Metro Police Department 22-23
Louisville Presbyterian Theological Seminary 102-103
Louisville Public Hospital /General Hospital 130-131
Louisville Public Warehouse Company 48-49
Louisville Science Center 68-69
Louisville Seed Company 72-73
Louisville Skyline 1, 2-3, 5, 6-7, 74-75
Louisville Slugger Field 44-45
Louisville Slugger Museum and Factory 70-71
Louisville Trust Bank 56-57
Louisville Trust Company 38-39
Louisville Water Company 114-115, 202-203
Main Street 8, 42-73
Mall St. Matthews 198-199
Market Street 30-41
Marriott Downtown Louisville Hotel 28-29
McAlpine Locks and Dam 140-141
Merchant and Manufacturers Building 150-151
Methodist Evangelical Hospital 135
Middletown 216-217
Model Drug Store 168
National City Bank 64-65
Neill-LaVielle Supply Company 62-63

Northwestern Parkway 140-143
Norton Healthcare Pavilion 135
Oatey-Forbes Drugs 166
Oertel's Brewery 212-213
Ohio Theater 98-99
Old State Fairgrounds 150-151
Olmsted Parks 12-13, 124-125, 148-149, 172-173, 178-179, 188-189
One Riverfront Plaza 56-57
Otis Hidden Company 62-63
Palace Theatre 96-97
Papa John's Cardinal Stadium, University of Louisville 239
Papa John's International, Inc. 236-237
Park DuValle Neighborhood 146-147
Pepsi-Cola General Bottlers 234-235
Plehn's Bakery 192-193
PNC Bank 24-25
Preiser Scientific 235
Presbyterian Seminary 102-103
Preston Hotel 54-55
Preston Street 134
Pryor's Restaurant 196
Qdoba Mexican Grill 169
Ramsi's Café on the World 167
Republic Bank & Trust Company 180-181
Rialto Theater 98-99
River Road 76-77, 222-223
Riverwalk 84-85
Robertson's Grocery 222
St. Francis High School 104-105
St. James Court 126-127
St. Matthews 190-199
Schuster Building 168-169
Second Street Bridge 50-51, 74-75
Seelbach Hotel 94-95
Seitz Drugs 210
Shawnee Park 148-149
Shelbyville Road 192-199
Sinking Fund Building 20-21
Snead Building 40-41
South Central Bell 100-101
Southern Bell Telephone and Telegraph 100-101
Spalding University 118-119
Speed, J.B. Art Museum 154-155
Standiford Field 156-157
Steam Engine Company No. 21 208
Stock Yards Bank 42-43
Stottman's Café & Grill 214
Straus, Herman & Sons 34-35
Temple Adath Israel 120-121
Theater Square 98-99
Third Street 114-115, 120-121
Transit Authority of River City (TARC) 112-113
Tyler Park 178-179
U.S. Bank 32-33
U.S. Marine Hospital 142-143
Union Station 112-113
United States Trust Company 66-67
University of Louisville Belknap Campus, Grawemeyer Hall 10
University of Louisville Health Sciences Center, Abell Administration Building 130-131
University of Louisville Hospital 132-133
University of Louisville Papa John's Cardinal Stadium 239
UPS Global Air Hub – Worldport 157-159
Uptown Theater 168
Vincenzo's 36-37
Vogue Theater 190-191
Waterfront 74-87
Waterfront Park 82-83
Whayne Supply Company 70-71, 150-151
Whiteside Bakery 144-145
Wine Rack 207
YMCA 104-105
YUM! Brands, Inc. Headquarters 227